Drupal 8 Quick Start Guide

Get up and running with Drupal 8

J. Ayen Green

BIRMINGHAM - MUMBAI

Drupal 8 Quick Start Guide

Copyright © 2018 Packt Publishing

Commissioning Editor: Amarabha Banerjee
Acquisition Editor: Reshma Raman
Content Development Editor: Roshan Kumar
Technical Editor: Shweta Jadhav
Copy Editor: Safis Editing
Project Coordinator: Hardik Bhinde
Proofreader: Safis Editing
Indexer: Tejal Daruwale Soni
Graphics: Alishon Mendonsa
Production Coordinator: Shraddha Falebhai

First published: October 2018

Production reference: 2021118

Published by Packt Publishing Ltd.
Livery Place
35 Livery Street
Birmingham
B3 2PB, UK.

ISBN 978-1-78934-031-0

www.packtpub.com

To Sasha, for making my life so much richer.

– J. Ayen Green

`mapt.io`

Mapt is an online digital library that gives you full access to over 5,000 books and videos, as well as industry leading tools to help you plan your personal development and advance your career. For more information, please visit our website.

Why subscribe?

- Spend less time learning and more time coding with practical eBooks and Videos from over 4,000 industry professionals

- Improve your learning with Skill Plans built especially for you

- Get a free eBook or video every month

- Mapt is fully searchable

- Copy and paste, print, and bookmark content

Packt.com

Did you know that Packt offers eBook versions of every book published, with PDF and ePub files available? You can upgrade to the eBook version at `www.packt.com` and as a print book customer, you are entitled to a discount on the eBook copy. Get in touch with us at `customercare@packtpub.com` for more details.

At `www.packt.com`, you can also read a collection of free technical articles, sign up for a range of free newsletters, and receive exclusive discounts and offers on Packt books and eBooks.

Contributors

About the author

J. Ayen Green is a software architect, developer, author, poet, and rascal. He is the author of titles including *Drupal 7 Views Cookbook*, *Drupal 6 Content Administration*, and *Drupal 6 Attachment Views*. Green enjoys nature, critters, photography, the arts, experiencing other cultures, riding horses, and discovering new ales. He and his wife, Sofia-Aileen, make their home in Atlanta when they're not traveling. Track him down `@accidentalcoder` or *theaccidentalcoder (dot) com*.

> *Thanks to the Editorial team at Packt for their assistance and support. I greatly appreciate their eye for detail and willingness to compromise. Thanks, too, to the technical reviewers who already know the material well yet tirelessly slogged through it to help better assure its accuracy.*

About the reviewers

Matt Glaman is an open source developer who has been working with Drupal since 2013, and doing web development for many years prior to that. Since then, he has contributed to over 60 community projects and has had 9 core commit mentions. While mostly focusing on Drupal and PHP development, Matt has created the ContribKanban.com AngularJS application to provide Kanban boards for the Drupal community to collaborate on. Currently, Matt is the US Team Lead at Commerce Guys.

John Bloomfield is a Software Engineer who lives in Oxfordshire, UK. He has been working in the web industry since 2002. He specialises in Drupal and is the Technical Director of JRB Digital Ltd. He has worked with Drupal since 2009 and has worked on some of the largest enterprise projects with BBC Studios, PwC, BrightLemon, CTI Digital, Atelier 7 and the Australian Government. At BBC Studios, he was part of the team that created BBC Store and also worked on the BBC Good Food and BBC Top Gear websites. John was the technical reviewer on a book by *Alex Burrows* called *Drupal 8 Blueprints*.

Alex Burrows is a web developer who specializes in Drupal and is based in Surrey, UK. He is the Technical Director of a UK-based agency called Digidrop, also based in Surrey, UK. He has worked with Drupal since 2008 and has worked on some well-known brands and large-scale projects; he is also very active within the Drupal community and attends every European and North American Drupalcon, where he is a mentor as well.

He is also one of the directors of DrupalCamp London CIC, which has been running since 2013, and he has been involved in the organization and its running since the beginning. Each year, it is becoming a bigger, better, and more popular event, and it has been marked as the second biggest Drupalcamp in the world. He is author of *Drupal 8 Blueprints*.

Packt is searching for authors like you

If you're interested in becoming an author for Packt, please visit `authors.packtpub.com` and apply today. We have worked with thousands of developers and tech professionals, just like you, to help them share their insight with the global tech community. You can make a general application, apply for a specific hot topic that we are recruiting an author for, or submit your own idea.

Table of Contents

Preface

Various terms are used to pigeon-hole Drupal: platform, framework, environment, and so on. At its core, Drupal is a content management system (CMS). Like the other terms, the meaning of CMS can be somewhat abstract and ambiguous, so here is what I feel the terms mean within the context of this book:

- **Content**: Digital material meant for sharing online
- **Management**: Manipulation for the sake of usability, continuity and viability, including creating, editing, storing, retrieving, indexing, searching, reviewing, moderating, and translating
- **System**: A cohesive collection of functionality

Put the three together, and you have Drupal at its heart: a *primarily used to make digital material available to users of the World Wide Web*.

Drupal offers a breadth and depth of capabilities, with a strong baseline functionality that's greatly expandable via a high degree of customization. There is a cost associated with this, and with any product that offers broad personalization, and that is a learning curve that is not insignificant. Think about your first interactions with a car's display console, a smart watch, or even the New York subway system, and you will likely recall an initial paralysis when deciding the first thing to do; for some, there is nothing intuitive in the experience.

My hope, and the goal of this book, is to ease your way into Drupal, demystifying the manner in which to accomplish the more common content management activities.

Who this book is for

This book is ideal for web developers who are looking to create professional web applications using Drupal 8. You should have some previous experience with Drupal and must have a basic knowledge of web application development in general. If you are looking to create fluent professional websites that will take you to the next level, then this book is for you.

What this book covers

Chapter 1, *Finding Your Way around Drupal*, will give you a step-by-step installation guide on creating a new Drupal site. You will also look at some of the major sections of the Drupal home page and administrative navigation.

Chapter 2, *Structuring Content Types*, will explore the fundamentals of Drupal content types and explains why we would want to create one. You will also look at content type fields, what they are, and what type fields are available. Gradually, you will also get to know how to create content types and add fields to content types as well.

Chapter 3, *Managing Users*, will brief you about users, covering all the major aspects of managing users, including roles and permissions for working with the content. You will also learn about the types of users and how Drupal can ensure limited access.

Chapter 4, *Creating and Editing Content*, will guide you through how to create and edit content. You will also learn how to configure the editor for various roles and how to define a custom URL for content as well.

Chapter 5, *Making Drupal Even More Useful*, will tell you what modules are, introduce their sources, and explain how to enable them. You will also explore a few of the more popular modules that extend Drupal's usefulness for users focused on content.

Chapter 6, *Grabbing Global Readership*, will tell you how to use Drupal's translation features. You will learn how to declare additional languages and how to enable the user to select their preferred language. You will also learn how to add icons that are used by site visitors and import user interface translations.

Chapter 7, *Feeding the Masses - RSS*, will tell you all about what an RSS feed is and how to create content meant for such a feed. You will also learn about the views module, what views are, and how to create a view with multiple feed displays.

Chapter 8, *Welcome Home!*, will guide you through how to improve a weak home page by editing its view, by providing an archive and recent content block, and by changing the footer menu.

To get the most out of this book

In order to work with Drupal 8, and to run the code examples found in this book, the following software will be required:

- Web server: Apache (recommended)
- Database: MySQL
- PHP

Download the color images

We also provide a PDF file that has color images of the screenshots/diagrams used in this book. You can download it here: http://www.packtpub.com/sites/default/files/downloads/9781789340310_ColorImages.pdf.

Conventions used

There are a number of text conventions used throughout this book.

CodeInText: Indicates code words in text, database table names, folder names, filenames, file extensions, pathnames, dummy URLs, user input, and Twitter handles. Here is an example: "Mount the downloaded WebStorm-10*.dmg disk image file as another disk in your system."

Bold: Indicates a new term, an important word, or words that you see onscreen. For example, words in menus or dialog boxes appear in the text like this. Here is an example: "Select **System info** from the **Administration** panel."

Warnings or important notes appear like this.

Tips and tricks appear like this.

Get in touch

Feedback from our readers is always welcome.

General feedback: If you have questions about any aspect of this book, mention the book title in the subject of your message and email us at customercare@packtpub.com.

Errata: Although we have taken every care to ensure the accuracy of our content, mistakes do happen. If you have found a mistake in this book, we would be grateful if you would report this to us. Please visit www.packt.com/submit-errata, selecting your book, clicking on the Errata Submission Form link, and entering the details.

Piracy: If you come across any illegal copies of our works in any form on the Internet, we would be grateful if you would provide us with the location address or website name. Please contact us at copyright@packt.com with a link to the material.

If you are interested in becoming an author: If there is a topic that you have expertise in and you are interested in either writing or contributing to a book, please visit authors.packtpub.com.

Reviews

Please leave a review. Once you have read and used this book, why not leave a review on the site that you purchased it from? Potential readers can then see and use your unbiased opinion to make purchase decisions, we at Packt can understand what you think about our products, and our authors can see your feedback on their book. Thank you!

For more information about Packt, please visit packt.com.

1
Finding Your Way around Drupal

This chapter will take you step by step through the Drupal site installation process. Following that, we will take a quick tour of the Drupal administration interface. During the course of this chapter, you will learn about the following topics:

- How to navigate the Drupal installation script
- How to log in to the Drupal administrative interface
- How to navigate and use the administrative interface
- Drupal-specific terms

Installing Drupal

Installing Drupal is a two-phase process. The first phase is the readying of the environment to host a Drupal website, and the second is running the installation script to create the website. Let's take a quick look at what Drupal is and the requirements for the first phase.

Readying the environment

Physically, Drupal is a collection of folders and files, most often found within a parent folder that is typically referred to as the Drupal root. Drupal also consists of a database, where the site's content and various settings are kept.

The Drupal root will most often be situated on a computer known as a web server that may contain many websites, though the web server could also exist on a laptop for use in developing websites. The environment in which Drupal exists will consist of the following:

- An operating system, which is usually Linux, but can be any another, such as Windows, OS X, or Unix
- A web server, such as Apache or Nginx
- A database, most often MySQL, which may be on the same server or on a separate database server
- The PHP language

The environment in which Drupal exists is collectively referred to as a LAMP environment, which stands for Linux, Apache, MySQL, and PHP, though other combinations exist, such as WAMP for Windows rather than Linux.

 The subject of the overall installation actions needed before running the Drupal site installation process, such as readying the LAMP environment, downloading the Drupal code, and installing the symbiotic technologies used with it, is outside the scope of this book.

To get started, an administrator should first have followed these steps, or similar:

1. Gone through the Drupal 8 installation (`https://www.drupal.org/docs/8/install/before-a-drupal-8-installation`)
2. Gathered the code (`https://www.drupal.org/docs/8/install/step-1-get-the-code`)
3. Installed the dependencies with Composer (`https://www.drupal.org/docs/8/install/step-2-install-dependencies-with-composer`)
4. Created a database (`https://www.drupal.org/docs/8/install/step-3-create-a-database`)
5. Configured the installation (`https://www.drupal.org/docs/8/install/step-4-configure-your-installation`)

Having done so, what exists now is the necessary environment for you to create your Drupal site. You might be thinking that the preceding steps have created the Drupal site already, but this isn't the case. Since I'm going to do this now, this is a good time to mention that my most often-used analogy of a website is a house. What the preceding steps did was select the location, prep the lot, run the utilities for it, pour the foundation, and ensure that you have the materials necessary to build the house. *Now*, we're going to build it.

"Oh, no!" you might be saying, "does that mean I need to learn all that web programming stuff, like HTML?" Fear not. One of the magical things that Drupal does is create all of the geeky stuff that's necessary for a website. After following a few steps, you will have a "vanilla" Drupal site, unadorned and not customized very much, but present and totally usable. Yes, just like a house that might be built in a cookie-cutter fashion, you have the ability to choose the paint, carpet, tiles, curtains, and appliances to make it unique and best reflect your vision, but those customizations are a topic outside of the scope of this book, although we *will* select a few "appliances" later on.

Unlike a house, there's no cutting, nailing, or other labor-intensive things to be done here with the raw materials waiting for assembly—just a few simple steps. First, though, there are a few pieces of information that you will need to know about in order to answer the questions that are asked about the new site during Drupal's installation process:

1. Which URL has been assigned to the site? If the site is on a remote server, it might be something with a familiar look, like `http://www.mysite.com`. On a local system, it could be something simple like `http://mysite` or even `http://localhost`.
2. What will the Drupal admin username and password be?
3. What will the email address for the site be?
4. What are the username and password for the database, and what is its name?

 If the site is not being accessed as a registered website, it is likely that an entry needs to be added to a file in your workstation's hosts file, which is the equivalent of a contact entry with the name you type and the address at which it can be found.

The installation process cannot be completed without the answers to these questions. Once you have them, we're ready to proceed!

We'll start by opening a browser. Any current version of the common ones, such as Chrome, Firefox, IE, Edge, or Safari, can be used. In the address bar, enter the URL that has been assigned to this site:

 The URL that I'll be using for this book is d8quickstart, and you will see this present in the address bar in any illustrations that contain one, such as image below. You will need to use the URL assigned for your site instead.

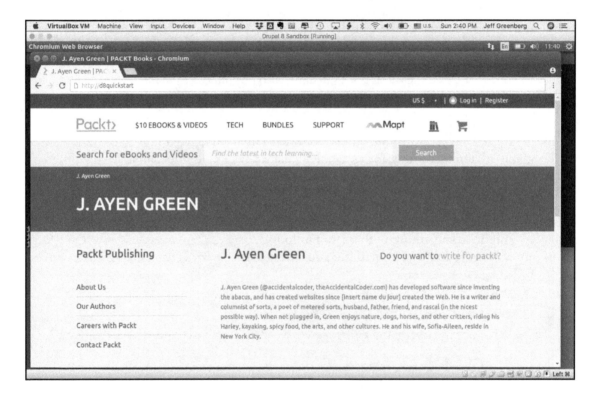

Running the Drupal installation script

This is the moment when you find out whether all of the pre-installation steps taken by your administrator were completed successfully. If so, you will see a screen similar to the following:

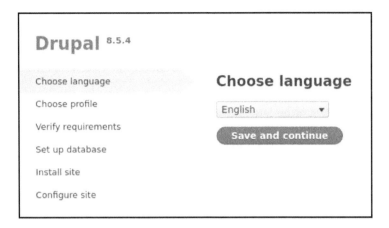

A variety of things can go awry at this point, and the reasons for this include the following:

- The web server entry is misconfigured or pointing to the wrong folder
- The URL doesn't match the one that was configured
- The host's entry for the URL is needed but is missing or has been mistyped
- The Drupal files aren't in the correct place, or the web server entry is pointing to the Drupal folder rather than the web/folder within it
- The file permissions are incorrect

Hopefully, you will receive the page shown in the preceding screenshot; if not, the preceding issues can be quickly resolved so that you can.

You will notice that the URL in the address bar is different than the one you entered. When Drupal determines that the site has not been installed, which in this case is determined by there being no viable database, it redirects the request for the home page (the URL you entered) to the installation page, located at `d8quickstart/core/install.php`.

Let's take a look at some of the things on this first screen. The Drupal version number is given at the top left of the page; this is **8.5.4** in my case. It is up to you regarding which version you install, but it should definitely be 8 dot something, and it is worth noting that installing older versions, such as installing 8.5.3 rather than the current (at the time of writing) 8.5.4, would risk using a version containing a security issue that has since been fixed.

The default installation language is shown.

You can select a different language than that presented. Drupal offers dozens, but do continue with English if you want your screens to match the examples that are used in this book.

Lastly, the list of steps down the left-hand side are not clickable because they are used as a progress indicator rather than a menu. As you proceed through the installation, the current step will be highlighted, just like **Choose language** is now. Let's move on by clicking the **Save and continue** button.

An installation profile is a configuration or collection of settings and software that's predetermined to be used for a specific purpose. Currently, Drupal has only three available in a normal installation: **Standard, Minimal**, and **Unami**, with Standard being the default setting, and the one we want. From here, click the **Save and continue** button.

If Drupal finds the files and folders that it needs to continue, it will move quickly past the **Verify requirements** step to **Set up database**. Otherwise, it will display a list of the issues that need to be addressed before it can continue. Some issues that frequently arise from steps during the pre-installation that were missed or performed incorrectly include the following:

- In the Drupal file folder structure, there is a default folder within a sites folder, and inside the default folder should be a files folder. It is not present in the Drupal installation files and needs to be created manually. Often, this step is missed, or the folder is created but in a way that will not allow Drupal to write to it.
- The default sites folder contains a file called `default.settings.php`. That file needs to be copied within the same folder and named `settings.php`. This, too, is often missed, or the file is present but will not allow Drupal to write to it.
- Missing PHP extensions, such as `ext-gd`. Messages of issues such as this should be referred to your server administrator.

Once things are as Drupal expects to find them, it will move on to inquiring about the database configuration:

It's time to make use of the database credentials that you obtained. In the text boxes provided, enter the database name, database username, and database password, and then click the Save and continue button.

At this point, Drupal will begin installing itself, entering configuration information into the database and initializing data structures. A meter will keep you informed of its progress, as shown in the following screenshot:

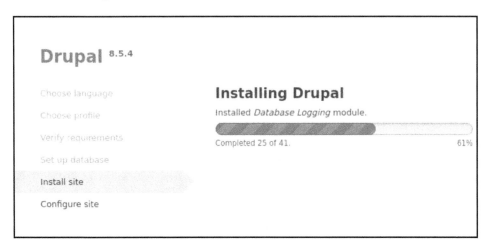

Once Drupal has installed itself, there is a final step in the process, that is, providing the site configuration. You will need the information that you obtained earlier to answer these questions:

Site information

The **Site name** that you enter will be the name Drupal identifies with the site, and the name that it will display if configured to show the site name rather than just a logo or logotype. This and any of the settings that you enter on this page can be changed at any time.

The **Site email address** is used to send contact messages when a contact form is enabled.

Site maintenance account

The capability to perform various tasks in Drupal is provided to a user by way of *permissions* that are granted, not by username, but by user *role*. We'll discuss this topic more in a later chapter. For now, the main thing you need to know is that the user role with the most capability is Administrator, and of the administrators, there is a single *superuser* login that is granted every permission. This role is most often referred to as *User 1* because this is always the first user that's configured for a site, and so receives that user ID.

The username, email address, and password entered here will be assigned to User 1. If this will not be you, and if you have not been given the credentials to use on behalf of the person it will be, make a note of the values that you enter so that they can use them to log in and change them.

Regional settings

Drupal creates log entries for certain events, and sends messages on behalf of the site, such as notifications of new content to subscribed users, login instructions for users receiving new accounts, and so on. The server itself might be located in one time zone, and may host several sites. The date and time on the computer might not necessarily be the same as that of the organization to which the site belongs. The location and time zone entered here are used to ensure that the log entries and communiques use the correct time.

Update notifications

Like any software, Drupal occasionally needs updating. Also, because much of its functionality comes via add-on modules and contributed modules, they occasionally need updating too, and each can have different update schedules or be updated on a completely ad hoc basis. Therefore, Drupal will perform a check on a daily basis to see if any new releases are available.

These checks are important, because the reason for the update can be to fix security-related issues. For that reason, it is normally good to keep the checkboxes checked. However, there are instances where there is no need to do so, for example, when there is an IT group that will be monitoring releases so that it isn't necessary for the site to do so, or in the case where the site is a local copy of a site used for development that will always match another site's versions. Again, the choices made here can be changed at any time, so if you're not certain, leave them selected.

Click the **Save and continue** button, and Drupal will render and display the new website for you!

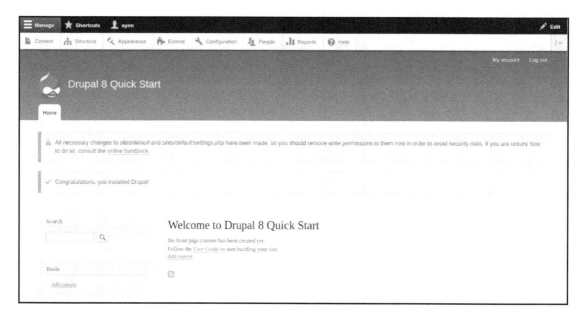

Congratulations! How was that for a quick start? You are looking at a fully functional Drupal site. However, what is a content management site without content? Are you ready to continue? Let's move on and give you the grand tour.

The behind-the-scenes tour

Like entering any complex location without a map in hand—a mall, a metro system, an amusement park—Drupal can be daunting to find your way around. So, throughout the rest of this chapter, I will be your tour guide, mapping out Drupal for you.

The home screen on a new site is presented to you via a *theme*. Themes control where elements appear on the page, their size, their color, and other aspects of the *user interface*, or UI. The default theme for Drupal 8 is called Bartik. It is important to remember that the homepage can (and likely will at some point) look somewhat or very different as a result of any of the following changing:

- Browser or browser version
- Device type (for example, an iPhone instead of a desktop computer)
- Theme
- Site's homepage layout
- User role permissions
- Items being added to or removed from the menus

So, try not to fixate on the exact location or appearance of the page elements, but rather develop an understanding of what they are so that you know where you want to go or what function you want, regardless of the appearance:

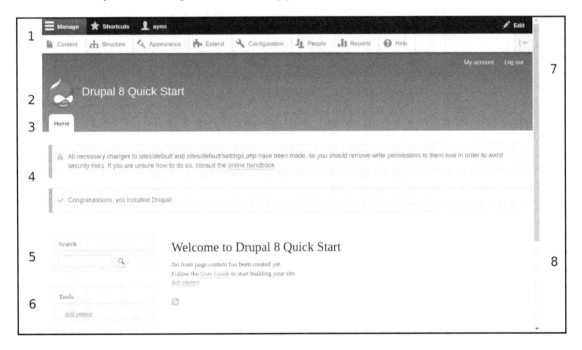

The preceding screenshots have numbers to the left and right that identify functional areas of the page. Each is identified in a key in the following table. A longer description will follow:

	Section
1	Administration menu
2	Branding
3	Tabs
4	System message area
5	Search widget
6	User menu
7	Main navigation
8	Content area

Administration menu

The administration menu, or admin menu, is typically only seen by users with the administrator role. Like any other Drupal menu, the entries displayed on it depend on the role of the user and the permissions assigned to that role. For example, someone with the role of editor might not see the choice for **Extend**, since that is associated with site administration.

The *Manage* link acts as a toggle that alternately shows or hides the row below it that contains links to the major administrative management pages.

The *Shortcuts* link replaces the administrative management links with links that the current user has added as bookmarks. For example, if by clicking links on successive pages you reach a page five clicks later, rather than doing that every time you want to go to that page, you can add it as a shortcut.

The final link in that row is one for the current user's account, which leads to the user page. The user page has tabs through which the user's account settings, including password, can be managed, as well as any shortcuts the user has added. Depending on the site and how it has been customized, this is often the page from which a user can reach the user profile and edit those fields. The fields and an explanation of them is as follows:

- **Content** leads to the content administration page on which content titles are listed and content can be managed. This will be covered more in `Chapter 4`, *Creating and Editing Content*.

- **Structure** leads to a further menu from which various site structures can be managed. Those of interest to content editors include content types and taxonomies, which are discussed in Chapter 2, *Structuring Content Types*.

- **Appearance** is where the installed site themes are listed and where they can be configured. A theme is a collection of files and settings that control the appearance of the site's pages. There are typically two themes that are applied to a site: the theme that visitors see, and the theme used for administrators accessing the site's backend.

- **Extend** leads to the module management section. Modules are add-ons for Drupal that provide additional functionality (see Chapter 5, *Making Drupal Even More Useful*). Here, modules can be installed and uninstalled.

- **Configuration** displays a menu of pages that serve as the primary administration portal, where many site settings are configured, such as the name of the site, which you provided during the install process. Here is a list of the various categories of settings, bearing in mind that the options presented are dependent on the user role:

  - **Account settings**: How user registration and account cancellation are handled, the content of system generated messages to users, whether a contact form is made available, and the role associated with site administrators.

  - **Text Format and Editors**: The restrictions on what content can contain (such as HTML tags) and which features the content editing tool provides to each user role (for example, you may not want someone who isn't an editor to be able to add links).

  - **Maintenance Mode**: The ability to set the site to prevent user login during maintenance activities.

  - **Configuration Synchronization**: The tool for importing or exporting the site configuration settings so that they can be transferred to or from another system.

  - **Search Pages**: For configuring site search, indexing settings, search logging, and adding site search pages

  - **URL Aliases**: For creating an alias for a specific page so that the default Drupal URL such as mysite.com/node/22 could be something more user friendly, such as mysite.com/using-drupal. I discuss an even better approach in Chapter 5, *Making Drupal Even More Useful*.

  - **RSS Publishing**: Configuration settings to provide a content feed from your site. We'll look at creating a selective RSS content feed in Chapter 7, *Feeding the Masses – RSS*.

- **Basic Site Settings**: Where the initial settings of site name, email address, and others can be changed.
- **Cron**: Drupal performs certain tasks in the background, meaning not via the browser, at defined intervals throughout the day. The interval can be configured here and an ad hoc request to run cron can be made.
- **Shortcuts**: As mentioned earlier, shortcuts allow you to place Drupal destinations on a task bar so that they can be reached with one click, and groups of them, such as those that apply to a singular purpose, can be managed here.
- **Filesystem**: Assets such as images, PDFs, and media files are kept in the web server's filesystem, and here is where their location is managed.
- **Image Styles**: Different configurations can be created that you can apply to uploaded images when the image is requested by the browser, depending on the context for their use, such as a cropped thumbnail for use in a list of items, or a full-sized version for use in a full page display of the content. An example of the use of an image style will be shown in Chapter 7, *Feeding the Masses – RSS*.
- **Image Toolkit**: If more than one system library for manipulating images (by the image style) is present, the selection of which to use can be made here.
- **Regional Settings**: For changing the locale and timezone settings that were selected or left unchanged during the installation process.
- **Date and Time Formats**: For setting the site default on how to display the date and time, an example of which is Monday, December 15, 2020 or Mon, 12/15/20.

As modules are added, the list of configuration pages shown in this section can grow:

- **People** is where user accounts, user roles, and user permissions are maintained, created, or in the case only of users and roles, removed. We will cover this in Chapter 3, *Managing Users*.
- **Reports** provide administrative reporting such as a site status report, as well as a report that shows the top search terms used on the site. Add-on modules can add further reports, as can Views, which we will use to add a report in Chapter 8, *Welcome Home!*
- **Help** provides getting-started tips, additional information about add-on modules that have help text associated with them, and other information.

Tabs

Tabs are a way of providing contextual information on a page rather than needing to leave the page to change context. For example, the default homepage has the Home tab as the sole context, but a page such as the user page might have a User tab that contains the user settings such as username and password, and a Profile tab for managing profile information such as country, gender, and social links.

System message area

The system message area is where important notices appear. Remember that the location could be different in another theme, as could the formatting. Unchanged, the location will be above the main page content, and the format will be one of the following:

- **Green**: General information worth noting
- **Yellow**: Indicating a warning; worth noting but not critical, usually meaning that the system completed what it was requested to do, but not without incident
- **Pink**: An error that should be acted upon or investigated, usually indicating that the system was unable to fulfil a request

These statuses are also used when a user completes a form, with the following as the typical presentation:

- **Green**: A message indicating that the form was saved or submitted
- **Yellow**: Inviting the user to review something in the content or to confirm its submission
- **Pink**: Indicating that a required field is without a value or that the value is not correct in context

Search widget

A content site would be of little value without the ability of the user to search for content based on one or more specific search terms or a phrase. So, some form of search widget is common, with a field in which to enter the term(s) and a link or button with which to initiate the search.

User menu

There can be actions or destinations specific to a user role or even a specific user, and a user menu is a good place to provide links to them. User menus are not always present, as often sites limit the navigation to a specific set that is woven into the theme.

Main navigation

The default main navigation consists of a link to the user's account page, which is sometimes represented with a silhouette or user image, and a link to log off though. Customizations can provide additional choices, as well. The main navigation can be much more prominent, such as in the case of e-commerce sites, where actions are as important to the user as the content itself.

Main content area

The heart of the CMS site is, after all, the content, and most homepages and interior pages will have an area in which to display content, whether that be text, video, or some other form of media. Depending on the theme, there could be initial content above and/or below the main content, more than one piece of content within the main content area, and small areas of additional content, blocks, in other parts of the page, such as the **Search** and **Tools** menus in the preceding screenshot.

Summary

In this chapter, we have learned how to run the Drupal installation script, which creates a new Drupal website. We also looked at the major sections of the Drupal homepage and administrative navigation.

In the next chapter, we will look at how content is stored, and how you can configure the system to store various types of content in a way that is meaningful to you and your site visitors.

Structuring Content Types

2

In `Chapter 1`, *Finding Your Way Around Drupal*, we learned what Drupal is and how to install it. This chapter will explore the fundamentals of Drupal content types, and the formats that define what information is saved with each piece of content. Upon reading this chapter, you will learn about content types and fields, creating a content type, adding fields to a content type, customizing the form used to enter content, and customizing the way the content is displayed.

What is content?

We all know what content is...sort of. This book is made up of content. This chapter contains content, as does this section within this chapter. The more important question is: what is it in the context of Drupal? This question is best answered with the home page as an example, because you'll know it when you see it!

The following screenshot shows a piece of content that I added to the site, in the main content area, with a thick rectangle around it:

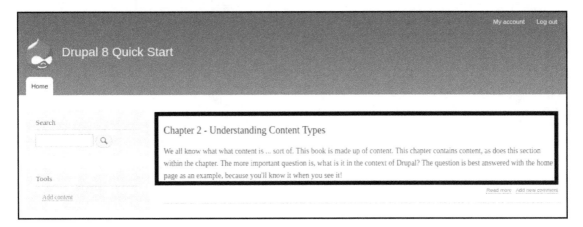

When rendered and displayed in the browser, it's simply content, but up until that point, it is content of a certain type, of a content type, also known in Drupal as a node bundle. Does Drupal look at this content simply as:

Chapter 2 - Understanding Content Types
We all know what content is ... sort of. This book is made up of content. This chapter contains content, as does this section within the chapter. The more important question is, what is it in the context of Drupal? The question is best answered with the home page as an example, because you'll know it when you see it.

No, content is stored within Drupal in a way that facilitates selecting it based on almost any criteria you wish.

Let's take a look at the database for a moment. This isn't something that you need to learn, but it's good for illustration purposes. If we were to look at the main identifying information for this piece of content within the Drupal database, we would see this:

```
+-----+------+---------+--------------------------------------+----------+
| nid | vid  | type    | uuid                                 | langcode |
+-----+------+---------+--------------------------------------+----------+
| 1   | 3    | article | 6166dc8e-1c64-4897-807e-7c535934f616 | en       |
+-----+------+---------+--------------------------------------+----------+
```

You can see this in the `article` value in the `type` column, which contains the content type in this table. "Article" is the content type of our content. Let's leave the database behind and look at our content and its content type in the way that you will use it, via the **user interface (UI)**.

 In the Drupal documentation, you will often find a URL specified in an abbreviated manner, omitting the domain name to avoid confusion since most users will be using different domain names, so instead of `mysite.com/page1` you might simply see `/page1`.

One of the pages used most often by a content editor is the content administration page. We'll begin there by clicking the **Content** link in the admin menu, which will take us to admin/content, as shown in the following screenshot:

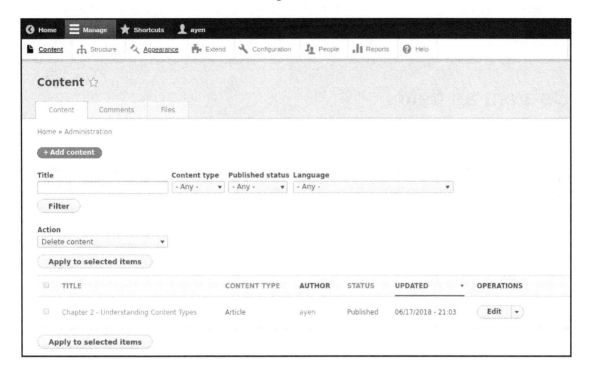

As you can see in the preceding screenshot, our content is listed, its title is on the left, and the type given is Article. We will learn more about the use of this page in Chapter 4, *Creating and Editing Content*, but for now we want to use it to lead us to the page on which we can edit our content. Let's click the **Edit** link at the opposite end of the row from the content title, which will display a node edit form for the content, as shown in the following screenshot:

Content as fields

We sometimes tend to think of content as a big block of body text, but content can be stored as discreet fields so that important elements can be easily accessed and properly formatted:

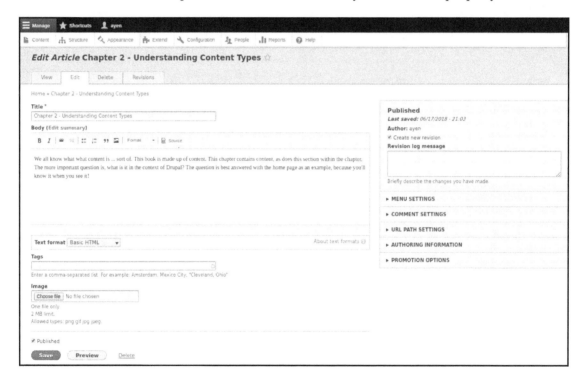

You can see the same content in this form as you did on the page. However, here you also see the fields that hold that content. The content title is in a field labeled **Title**, and the main text is in a field labeled **Body**. There are two additional fields that are not being used by this particular piece of content: a field for categories, labeled **Tags**, and one that is used for attaching an image to the content, labeled **Image**.

By having a Title field and a Body field, both the user and Drupal understand that the information in each is separate from the other. This doesn't mean that they cannot be displayed together, but there are many reasons why we may want to be able to differentiate them.

For example, when this content was displayed on the homepage, the title and the body text were formatted differently. Another example is that we might want to have Drupal provide us with a list of content titles. In both examples, it is important for Drupal to be able to determine which part of the content *is* the title. If all of the content in the piece was thrown together, there would be no way for Drupal to know where the title ends and the body text begins. Having them in separate fields removes any ambiguity.

So, we have seen what the content looks like when separated into separate fields. But where do the fields come from? How does Drupal know which fields to offer to receive our input? Let's take a look at that next.

Understanding content types

A content type is essentially a collection of fields used to hold the various items that together form the whole of the content. In the case of the piece of content that we have been using, it is an example of the **Article** content type, which is one of the two content types that are present when you first create a new Drupal site, with the other being the **Page** content type.

If you think of a company's job application, every application contains the same fields for entering information, even though the information differs from one to another. In this example, the job application is a content type. Let's take a look at the Article content type in terms of how Drupal provides it.

To navigate via the admin menu, click **Structure**. Then, on the next page, click **Content types**, which will lead to a page that you can also reach via the browser instead at /admin/structure/types, as shown in the following screenshot:

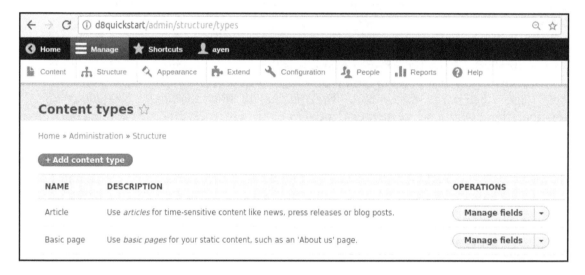

Defining the content type

We'll now take a look at the content type definition. To start, rather than click on the default choice of **Manage fields**, click the arrow next to that and select **Edit**:

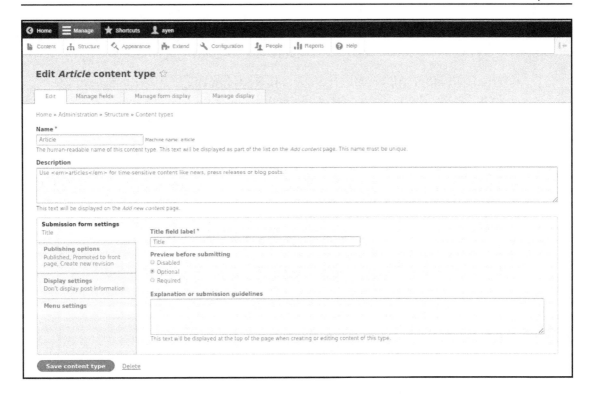

Let's take a brief look at the settings in the preceding form:

- **Name**: This is the plain language name that the content type will be identified with. In this case, this is **Article**. To the right of this human-readable name is what is referred to as the **Machine name**, which is the internal name. This is generated automatically by Drupal, and is usually the lowercase version of the name, with multiple words having spaces replaced by an underscore.
- **Description**: This is a place to describe the purpose of the content type and, perhaps, rules of its usage. The descriptive text entered here will be displayed along with the content type name when given a list of available content types to choose from when creating content.

Following these two fields is a series of vertical tabs that provide additional configuration items.

Submission form settings

The submission form is the form with which content is created:

- **Title field label**: All content has some identifying key that also acts as a title when the content is displayed. The default is to refer to this value as the *Title*, but in some cases, this may not be appropriate. For example, with a content type that defines travel destinations, the title would work better as *Destination* or *Location* than *Title*. This field is required. Its value will be used as the prompt on the entry screen when creating a piece of content of this type.
- **Preview before submitting**: When creating or editing content, it is likely that the content, as viewed in the editor, will differ from the content as viewed on the web page. Previewing provides the latter view. The selection here will determine whether previewing is available, and if so, whether it will be optional or required to do so before submitting.
- **Explanation or submission guidelines**: This is simply a place to enter a description that will be shown to the person creating or editing the content.

Publishing options

Typically, content is entered in a rich text editor window in a form. Since this entry can very well be the first draft of that content, it may not be desired to have it published immediately. Some content types will be of this type, more often than not, while others, such as one that contains only a title and URL, will not require more than one draft. Because of this, publishing options are provided. Here, in the content type form, the default choice for these options can be set:

- **Published**: If selected, the content will be published as soon as it is saved
- **Promoted to front page**: Not all content is necessarily intended for the homepage, and a piece of content having this value set, or not, can be used to determine whether it should appear there

In Drupal, the site's homepage is sometimes referred to as the *front page*, like in a newspaper.

- **Sticky at top of lists**: When no other scheme is put in place, the front page displays a specified number of article teasers, and as more content is created, the older ones "drop" off the page. If a piece of content is meant to remain on the page while others cycle on and off, such as a welcome message, it can be accomplished by setting this value.
- **Create new revision**: Imagine making changes to content, saving them, and realizing that something was changed that shouldn't have been. What do you do? The original version is gone! Or is it? When a new revision is created, it contains the content as it existed before the changes were made. Should the need arise, the current version can be reverted to that of the revision, providing a complete undo.

Display settings

Display author and date information: whether to set this or not depends on the type of content that will be displayed and the look that's desired for the site.

Menu settings

Sometimes, it is desirable to add a piece of content to a menu, particularly if it is somewhat static on the site. For example, Terms and Conditions would be persistent site content, whereas a notice about the current week's activities would not. The former might be one of a specific content type, perhaps **Legal**, and you might desire that every piece of such content be listed in the **Footer** menu. In this example, the **Footer** within the list of **Available menus** would be checked, and if there were a heading, **Legal**, already in that menu, it could be selected as the **Default parent item**. In that case, all content of that type would, by default, be added to the **Footer** menu as child content to **Legal**:

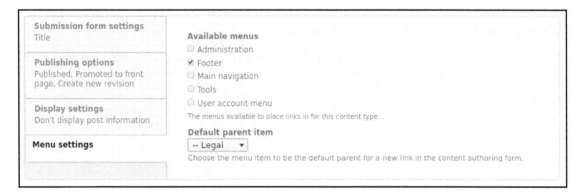

More on menus will be found in Chapter 8.

That completes the main form for content types. We will be creating a new content type later in this chapter. For now, let's move on to managing content type fields.

Managing content type fields

A field can be thought of as a container that you put something in, that something in our context being content. Why do content types have fields rather than one big box in which to put the content, like a page in MS Word? Let's consider an example.

Suppose our content is related to appointments. Ms. Jones is making an appointment. One possibility is that the appointment is entered as text, like so:

January 20 at 1:30 PM Ms. Jones will see Mr. Kim to discuss investments.

All of the information needed is there. However, what happens when a list is needed of all the appointments for the next two weeks? Or when a list of all Ms. Jones's appointments are needed? Or when a decision is made to change the date format on all appointments? In those cases, having the information in a form that is difficult to aggregate, search, or edit globally is problematic.

What if the appointments were stored like a spreadsheet?

Date/Time	Client	Seeing	Reason
January 20, 2018	Ms. Jones	Mr. Kim	Investment discussion

With the information segregated into meaningful pieces, it is much easier to find what is needed and edit it. That is the idea behind fields.

We've been working with the **Article** content type. Let's take a look at how its fields are defined. At the top of the current page, we'll click on the **Manage fields** tab:

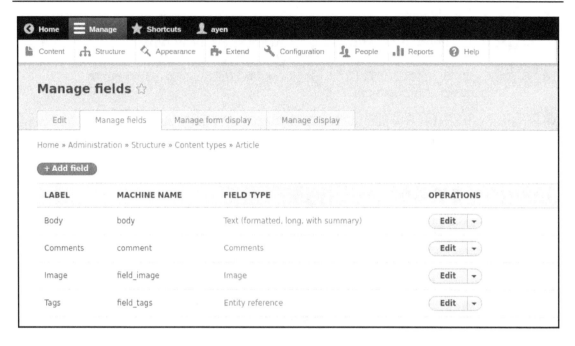

We saw the title field on the content type form. This screen is for optional fields. There could be no additional fields for the content type at all, but since all content types must have a title field, whatever its label, it isn't included here.

When we looked at the content edit form, we saw the title and body fields. The body field is listed here. The field is of a type meant to hold text without any specific use or format in mind. We'll be looking more at field types when we create a new content type later in this chapter.

The comments field is meant to hold a comment about the content. There may be several instances of this field, one for each comment created. A comment is actually a content entity type on its own, and so even though the comments are seen when viewing the article's content, the actual contents of the comment field is simply the ID of the comment.

The image field is used for displaying an image along with the content, allowing an image to be uploaded. The image field is a reference of the information needed to retrieve the actual image from where it is stored, and the article image field, if an image is being used, will contain the address of that record.

The final field is for tags. Think of tags as categorical information that can be used for searching for the content. This is using another reference field type like comments and images, that is, taxonomy. We will be looking at taxonomy more in Chapter 7.

Taxonomy is a content structure, referred to as an *Entity* in Drupal. Another type of entity is a *User*. Article is a content type, also known as a *Bundle*, which is a sub-type of an Entity type known as a *Node*. Bundles can include Article, Page, Blog post, and other types of content that's intended for readers.

We can look at the other two tabs at the top of the page, **Manage form display** and **Manage display** when we create a content type. In fact, let's do that now!

Designing a content type

We've already taken a look at the *Article* content type. It contains a title and a place to enter text, and allows the addition of an image and category tags. So, with all that, why would you want to create a content type? Well, because vanilla is a nice flavor, but not the <u>only</u> flavor!

We need an appointment list. Well, not really, but we're going to need an example of a type of content that is nothing like an article, and an appointment is a good example of that.

The first thing to do after determining that a new content type is needed is designing it. Looking back at the Article content type, it had settings and fields. So will this one. It helps to decide in advance what those will be in order to create a design, so let's do that. We'll use two forms for the design – nothing fancy, just lists to refer to when entering information into the content type forms.

Content type settings

Setting	Value
Name	Appointment
Description	Appointment information
Title field label	Name
Default options	Published Promoted Sticky Revision

With this content type, we will pretend that we are in an office that gives appointments to its clients. The content type *Name* and *Description* values are self-evident.

The *Title field* label will be Name, since it will contain the name of the person who has the appointment.

The selected Default options will be *Published* and *Revision*. We are selecting *Published* because we want appointments to be active and set as soon as they are saved.

Promoted is not set because we don't want the appointments to be displayed on the front page like an article, nor do we want the most recently entered appointment to be the one shown. We will want the appointment nearest to the current date and time to be shown.

Sticky is not set because we have no need for any appointment to remain on the front page.

Finally, we do set *Create new revision*, so that any time an appointment is changed, Drupal will save the previous version rather than simply overwriting it.

We will make no changes to the default settings on the other tabs since they meet our needs, and so they do not appear in the list. With our list complete, on the administrative menu, we can click **Structure**, then **Content types**, and then the +**Add content type** button, which will lead us to the page at /admin/structure/types/add. Once there, enter the information from the form, and after ensuring that the *Default options* settings are as they should be, as shown in the following form, click the **Save and manage fields** button:

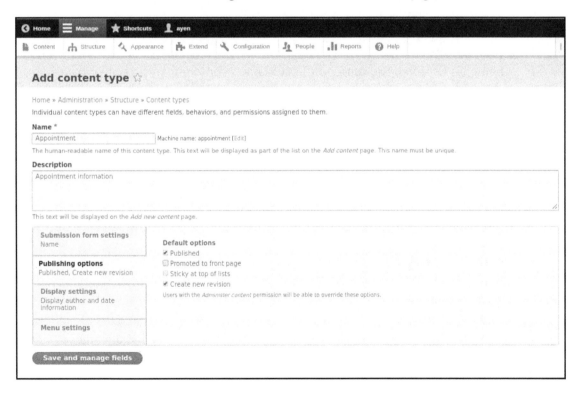

Fielding the content type

So far, we have created the *Appointment* content type. At this point, it could be used for creating content. However, it is not yet constructed to fulfil its purpose. It only has two fields, one being the title, Name, and the other a field for body text, of which there will be none with this content type. We will need to do a little work to make this content type usable for our purpose.

In order to add the necessary fields to the content type, it would be helpful to know what the choices are.

Field types

A fresh installation of Drupal contains a number of field types that are ready to use, and a few that first need to be enabled in order to be used:

GENERAL FIELDS:

- **Boolean**: Can have only two values, such as Yes/No, On/Off or, with one value being understood, such as Completed. This is commonly represented by a checkbox
- **Date**: Displays a date in whatever format is configured
- **Email**: Accepts text formatted as a valid email address
- **Link**: Accepts text formatted as a valid URL and the text that will be clicked
- **Timestamp**: A long numeric value that stores a date, time, and time zone

NUMERIC FIELDS:

- **Number (decimal)**: A value that can have numerals before and after the decimal point
- **Number (integer)**: A value that contains no fractional portion
- **Number (float)**: A value that requires a large number of decimal positions and great precision
- **List (float)**: A floating point number that must match one from a list of values
- **List (integer)**: An integer value that must match one from a list of values

REFERENCE FIELDS (fields that refer to other content):

- **Content**: A reference to another piece of content, of one of the content types configured for use with the field
- **Comments**: Used for accepting comments about the content
- **File**: A reference to a file that was uploaded to the system, such as a PDF

- **Image**: A reference to an uploaded image, such as a JPG or PNG
- **Taxonomy term**: A value or set group of information among others of a common category (taxonomy), such as tags, countries, months, and so on
- **User:** A reference to a user account
- **Other**: A reference to a custom type of entity (other than those mentioned previously)

TEXT FIELDS:

- **List (text)**: A text field whose value must be one of a provided list
- **Text (formatted)**: Text of a short length that can be formatted, such as being bold, italic, and so on
- **Text (formatted, long, with summary)**: Text that can be formatted, lengthy, and can have a separate summary for use as an abbreviated teaser
- **Text (plain)**: A short piece of text that will not have any formatting
- **Text (plain, long)**: Text that will not have any formatting and can be lengthy

FIELDS REQUIRING ENABLING:

- **Address**: An address field that can be configured based on the country to which the address applies and the fields desired
- **Computed Field**: A field that can be tied to programming to determine a certain value
- **Datetime Range**: Stores a beginning and ending date in whichever format is needed
- **Entity Reference Revisions**: Provides a reference to an entity and also provides for the storing of revisions whenever the entity is modified
- **Simple Google Maps**: Provides the ability to display a link to a Google map or a one-line address as a Google map
- **Telephone**: For holding a validly formatted phone number

These are the fields that are available from a new Drupal installation. As additional modules are added, this list can grow.

Our content type field

You can see from the preceding lists, there are fields for most of the various types of information that you will need to store. It's not just a matter of the type of data, like text or number, but often what information the data represents, like a phone number or URL, and that's because there is often programming code that provides the formatting or validates what has been entered. For example, entering an email address in a phone number field will cause an error to be displayed.

So, let's take a look at a list of the information that we will want to store for an appointment, and the type of field that we can use for that. We'll also decide on a name for each field, which will be used for its label on the entry form, and help text with a a description to remind us or inform other users about the field's use:

Information needed	Field type	Label	Help Text
Client name	text (plain)	Name[1]	
Client phone number	text (plain)[2]	Phone	###-###-####
Client email address	email	Email	For example, `bill@gmail.com`
Appointment date and time	date	Date	
Who the appointment is with	list (text)	With	Select a name
The purpose of the appointment	text (plain, long)	Reason	
The status of the appointment	list (text)	Status	Select a status

[1] This is the renamed Title field

[2] There is a field type for telephone number, but it is not enabled, so we will use plain text

With our list prepared, it's time to create the fields for our content type.

Adding fields to the content type

Still on the **Manage** *fields* page (`/admin/structure/types/manage/appointment/fields`), let's first make a change to the one existing field: Body. We will not have body text in this content type, so:

1. Click the arrow next to **Edit**
2. Select **Delete**
3. confirm the deletion

With that done, click the **+Add field** button.

We'll add the fields shown in the preceding order for the most part. The page we see now has two dropdown select widgets: one for creating a new field, and one for reusing a field on this content type that already exists.

Keeping in mind that the Name field already exists in our content type, being the renamed Title field that all content types contain, the first field we will add is Client phone number:

1. Click on the **Add a new field** dropdown
2. Scroll down and select **Text (plain)** from the list.

A new field, **Label**, appears, and is marked with a red asterisk, indicating that it is required that you type something in the field:

- The label, as found in our preceding table, will be **Phone**

Having entered the label, you will notice that to the right of the field that a **Machine name** appears. The machine name is the name by which Drupal will identify the field. Once you save the field, the label can be changed at any time, but the field name will not change, because it will already have been *set in stone* within the database. Were you to desire a specific machine name, now is the time it can be changed, by clicking the **Edit** link. You would be able to edit the name, keeping in mind that there are some naming rules, such as needing to use underscores rather than hyphens, and that the **field_** prefix cannot be removed. We have no need to override the field name:

- Click **Save and continue**

A new page is loaded, which is for defining the field storage. Fields in Drupal have three components: the *definition*, which describes the field, the *storage*, which defines how the field will be stored in the database, and the actual *contents* of the field for a given piece of content, when that content is created.

The first field is **Maximum length**, and is required. For this field type, a standard (as opposed to long) text field is desired. The default is 255, meaning that the field can hold up to 255 characters. It's alright if less are entered when the content is created. You need only change this value if the contents should be of a particular length and no more. In the case of the phone field, it depends. If all client contacts will be local, or at least domestic, then it would be alright to limit the length to match the structure of your phone numbers. For example, in the U.S., phone numbers are ten digits. That said, the length of such a phone number can be greater than ten digits if entered with a format such as (212) 555-1212. So, be careful when limiting the length. We'll just leave it at 255.

The **Allowed number of values** field defines whether a piece of content, an appointment in this case, can contain more than one occurrence of this field. We have the option to leave it as **Limited** to one value, or change the number to another specific quantity, or click the dropdown widget and selecting **Unlimited** to indicated any number of instances of this field can be created. We want to be able to take two contact numbers for the client in case the need to contact them arises and attempts of using the first number are not successful:

1. Change the 1 to 2
2. Click **Save field settings**

The third, and final, page in the field creation process is now displayed. If we want to change the storage settings that we just saved, we could click the **Field settings** tab and do so.

 The storage settings for a field can not be changed once content has been created that uses that field, unless all such content is first deleted. Attempts to click this tab after content has been created will result in a display of the settings with a message indicating that they can no longer be changed due to content existing.

The first field in the form is for the **Label**. This is the value that we entered earlier. It can be changed now if we have since decided on a new name. The **Machine name** can no longer be changed.

The contents of the **Help text** field, if any, will be displayed on the content form beneath the field you are creating. We'll use the entry from our table to provide the content creator with a hint as to the field contents, which in our case is the format of the phone number used locally:

• Enter ###-###-#### in the **Help Text** field

The **Help Text** field can contain HTML, as indicated by its own help text. For example, we could elaborate on our description by instead entering the following:

Enter a phone number with the format ###-###-####

Which would be displayed as follows:

Enter a phone number with the format ###-###-####

The next field in the form is the **Required** field. If this box is checked, the field will appear in the content form with its label containing whatever formatting is defined for a required field in the site theme. By default, this would be a red asterisk, as we see in the current form beside **Label**.

If a field is required, content cannot be saved unless a value has been provided for the field. Be careful not to require a field that could legitimately be left empty. Examples of this are a zip code or post code for an optional address, a list of options where none may apply, or a checkbox, where empty indicates "no".

In our case, we will leave the phone field as not being required. The final field is for a default value. Of course, a phone number field is unlikely to have a default value, given that we have no idea what the value will be. There are circumstances where a default value makes sense. For example, if we have a grouping of address fields, one of which is Country, and if most of the entries will be from the United Kingdom, it would make sense to offer it as a default value rather than forcing the user to scroll down a list of countries to the U's.

 If you provide a default value, be prepared for erroneous content due to users accidentally leaving the field untouched and saving the form with the default value.

We will leave the form containing no default value:

- Click **Save settings**

At this point, we have saved our first field configuration, **Phone**. Technically, the field does not exist until content is created using this field, but its definition and configuration exist at this point. You can see that our content type field list for the **Appointment** content type has changed, with *field_phone* having been added to it.

We will follow the same process for each of the remaining fields in our table. For each of them, I note any considerations for their storage and configuration settings, as follows:

Date: **date** field type – the checkbox for **Required** should be checked.

With: **list (text)** field type – in the **Allowed values list** box, add 2-3 names in the form last name, first name, one person per line. As an example, I have added the following:

Jones, Janet
Smith, Steve

Status: **list (text)** field type – in the **Allowed values list** box, add the following:

pending
active
canceled
completed

And in the *Default Value* dropdown, select **pending**.

Having created all of the fields in our table, the **Manage Fields** page should look as follows:

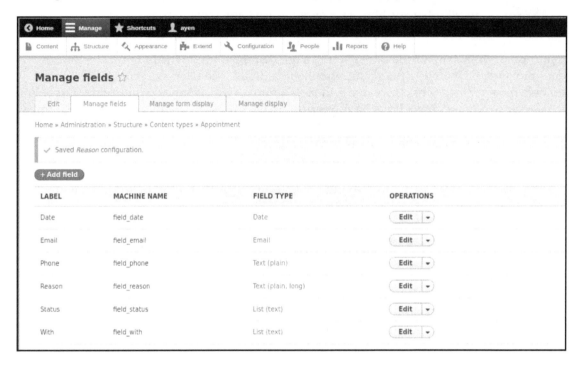

Summary

In this chapter, we have learned the following: firstly, what a content type is, and then why we would want to create one. Furthermore, we looked at content fields, found out what they are, and looked at what field types are available. Then, we moved on and looked at how to design and create content types, before finally finishing by adding fields to our content types.

- What a content type is
- Why we would want to create a content type
- What content type fields are
- Which field types are available

- How to design a content type
- How to create a content type
- How to add fields to the content type

We will return to our content type later in this book when we learn about creating content for it, configuring the content creation form, and designing the way the content is displayed.

 We added fields to a new content type in this chapter. It is also possible, using the same administrative pages, to edit existing content types and add new fields to them, change existing fields, and remove fields that are no longer needed.

In the next chapter, we will learn about administering users, their roles, and the permissions assigned to those roles.

3
Managing Users

In `Chapter 2`, *Structuring Content Types*, we learned how content is stored as a type, about content types, the fields that comprise them, and how to create a custom content type.

This chapter is all about the reason for having a Drupal site, or any website for that matter: users.

If no one were accessing the site's content, there would be little reason for having the site, right? However, not all access is alike. You're going to learn about user types and how Drupal provides a way for you to ensure that no one has more access than they require. More specifically, this chapter covers the following topics:

- User types
- User roles
- User permissions
- Creating a user

User types

In the context of a **Content Management System** (**CMS**), a user is simply someone who uses the site. If that were all there is to it, if everyone were always the same in the *eyes* of Drupal, we could stop right here. So, you won't be surprised to read that all users are not necessarily the same. Of course, I'm not referring to the personal aspects of the users when I write that; I mean that users are not necessarily all the same in terms of their reason for accessing the site and what ability they are given to do so.

If we look at USERS as a top-level classification with the thought of further classifying them, doing so depends on a choice: are we classifying them in a real-world sort of way, or as Drupal does? In the following table we see them compared:

USERS		
Administrative	**Creative**	**Consumer**
Focus on the configuration and settings of the site rather than site content.	Focus on site content	Availers of site content

From the real-world point of view, we tend to categorize users based on their functional relationship with the site. If you think of these relationships in the context of a home, some might simply live there and consume food (think teenagers), some will contribute to the look and contents of the home, and others will be responsible for maintaining it. Yes, a user can appear in more than one category, as shown in the following table:

USERS		
Administrative	**Authenticated**	**Anonymous**
Authenticated + permission to perform higher level activities.	Anonymous + a login to access privileged functionality or content.	Some access to the account as an unknown site visitor.

From the Drupal point of view, it pretty much comes down to what you will be allowed to do on the site and whether you require an account to do so. For example, some sites allow unknown site visitors to read the content and comment on it. Others only allow access to the content for them without commenting, and others do not allow anonymous access at all. Returning to the analogy of a home, those who can do whatever they like to it have administrative access; those who are allowed to enter have authenticated access, albeit with different "roles", such as friends versus residents; and those who come to the front door (if there is no gatekeeper or doorman preventing that) who are unknown are anonymous.

For the most part, *Consumer* users are *Anonymous*, with some premium or secure content requiring them to be *Authenticated*. *Creative* users are typically *Authenticated*. And *Administrators* are usually always, *Administrative*. The takeaway is this: sites vary, and so does the segregation, if any, of user types.

User roles

To Drupal, a *role* has the same meaning as it does outside of Drupal: the functional aspect of the user, sometimes considered a *persona*. It's worth mentioning that Drupal does blur the line a bit between a role and a user type, because it comes with three roles predefined, and they are the user types mentioned earlier. While *administrator* makes sense as a role, *authenticated* and *anonymous* are not really roles, but appear there to simplify things, for administrators, at least.

So, let's take a look at the default user roles inside of Drupal before we move on to discussing why you would want additional ones. If you are using the menus, click **People** in the **Admin** menu (`admin/people`), and then click the tab labeled *Roles*, as in the following:

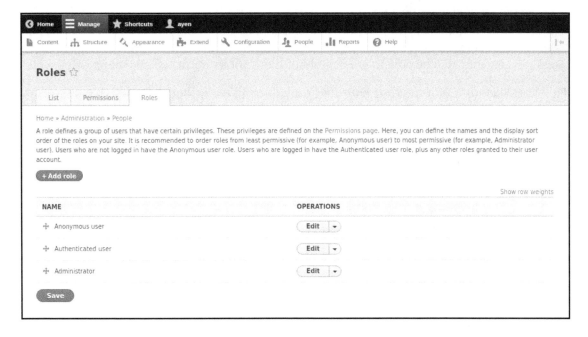

The preceding screenshot shows the roles that are predefined in Drupal. I disagree with the given description of a role, because it is unclear. The order of operation in Drupal is that privileges are assigned to roles, and roles are assigned to users. We'll discuss that more when we add a user and when we assign some permissions, later in this chapter.

For now, let's focus on the default Drupal roles themselves. As I mentioned earlier, *anonymous* and *authenticated* are actually more user types than roles, but in Drupal they are referred to as roles. When would these three roles, alone, be sufficient? One example would be a site where all users with logins can create content, and all users that have no login can only view that content. If those are the limits to your organizational and site complexity, you can jump ahead to the section on *User Creation* if you'd like.

Let us consider. The anonymous role stands on its own. Why? Because it is defined as a user with no account or login, which is to say, a user that is not identified. We would not assign the role of *Anonymous* to a user account, because if there is an account, the user of it is no longer anonymous. There would be no sense in creating different roles for anonymous users, because there would be no user accounts to assign those roles. So, that leaves us with the other two roles, and we can use those to derive examples.

On our site, we will have four types of non-administrative authenticated users. The first will be authenticated users in general. That is, users with this role will be able to login, and in addition to being able to see the **Article** and **Page** site content that **Anonymous** and all users can see, they will be able to see content of the **Appointment** type we defined, as well.

This could be our use of the Authenticated role, since all users logging in will have those capabilities at a minimum, but we won't use that role for it. Why? Because we have to account for the possibility that later there might be the need to have some users who can log in but cannot access appointment data. In general, I prefer to leave the predefined roles unchanged for that reason...use them as a model instead, or as is. So, we will call the new role **Client**.

 One thing to keep in mind when creating new roles for a logged-in user is that because the user is logged in, and thus also an authenticated user, the user will receive all the permissions assigned to the **Authenticated** role, too.

There will be three additional roles for authenticated users on our site: **Client**, who is able to view appointments; **Consultant**, who is able to create and edit appointments; and **Editor**, who is able to create and edit content other than appointments. The complete list of our user roles and their use are given in this table:

Role	Use
Anonymous	Unknown users. Able to read *Article* and *Page* content.
Authenticated	Users with accounts. Able to comment on *Article* content.
Client	Authenticated + able to view *Appointment* content

Consultant	Authenticated + able to perform *Appointment* CRUD[*]
Editor	Authenticated + able to perform *Article* and *Page* CRUD[*]
Administrator	Authenticated + able to access Drupal admin functions and manage user accounts

* CRUD = Create/Read/Update/Delete

Follow these steps to add the **Client** role:

1. Click the **+Add role** button, which leads to the page `admin/people/roles/add`
2. Enter the *role name*, `Client`
3. Click **Save**

Notice that the role list now includes **Client**. Follow the steps above for the **Consultant** and **Editor** roles as well. The role list should now appear as shown in the following screenshot:

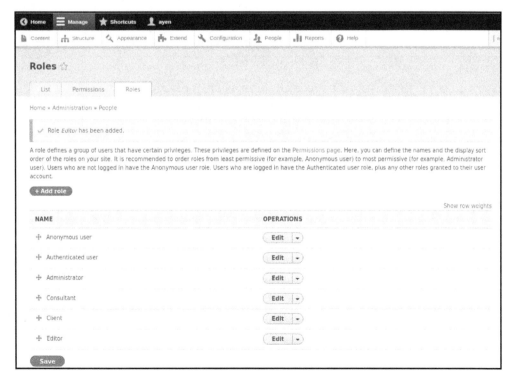

All roles are now available for use. However, their capabilities have not yet been defined. Since we've covered all that we need to regarding the creation of roles, let's move on to the topic of permissions.

Managing permissions

Any page element that a user can view or hear or otherwise interact with, such as a menu link, is available for doing so because the user, via a role, has been given permission to do so. This is a very important concept, so I will give an example. You have no doubt seen a *Terms and Conditions* link on most sites.

On a Drupal site, if you see such a link, it is because your user role has been granted permission to access that content (the **Terms and Conditions** page). Were that permission not granted for your user, the link would probably not be visible. Were it still visible, or were you to enter the URL for the page in your browser, you would receive a message stating that you have not been granted access to that content.

Because permissions can be granular and detailed, there are a lot of them, and adding modules will typically add more to the list. We're going to focus on a subset of them to keep things simple.

With that warning, let's take a look by clicking the **Permissions** tab at the top of the page, which will take us to `admin/people/permissions`.

The structure of the permissions page is all permissions provided in a scrollable table. Across the top of the table are the roles defined on the site. You'll see that they are the same as those that were listed earlier. Down the left-most column of the table is the list of permissions for actions categorized by alphabetical topic and/or name of the module that defines them.

The manner of management is quite simple. If a box is checked, that column's role has the listed permission. For example, looking at the first permission, which is associated with the *Block* module, the ability to *Administer blocks* has been granted only to those users having the **Administrator** role.

Rather than scroll down and up for each of the roles, we'll approach this by permission, so that we only have to scroll once. In the following table, I will provide each of the categories and permissions within it that require our attention, as well as what the checkboxes should look like after you have checked the appropriate ones to accomplish the grants we defined earlier for our roles.

We will not be changing any of the settings in the **Administrator** column, but I have included it so that the relative position of each role is as you see it on your screen.

I will only provide rows for those permissions that require a setting change. For example, you will notice under the category of Comment that already all authenticated user types have the ability to post comments, while Anonymous users have the ability to view comments, so no changes are needed, which is why that row won't appear in this table:

Category/Permission	Anonymous User	Authenticated User	Administrator	Client	Consultant	Editor
NODE						
Appointment: Create new content			X		X	
Article: Create new content			X			X
Appointment: Delete own content			X		X	
Article: Delete own content			X			X
Article: Edit any content			X			X
Appointment: Edit own content			X		X	
Article: Edit own content			X			X
Access the Content overview page			X		X	X
View own unpublished content			X		X	X

Most of the permissions in the preceding table relate to CRUD operations on specific content types. That is, being able to create (add), edit (update) and delete content of a specific type, such as the *Appointment* type that we created. You can see that we granted permission to perform such operations to Consultants, but not to Editors, whereas we granted permission to perform those same operations on *Article* content to Editors, but not to Consultants.

Access rights, permissions, take effect immediately. That is, even if you have permission to perform a certain action or access a type of content, were that permission to be removed from your role, your access to that action/content would then be gone, unless and until it is reinstated.

You will notice that some of the permission descriptions look very similar, such as:

- Appointment: Edit own content
- Appointment: Edit any content

The difference between the two is that with the second, the user is able to edit Appointment content regardless of who created it, whereas with the first, the user needs to have created it.

The final permission, *View own unpublished content*, is worth noting as well. Unless this permission is granted, if a new piece of content is saved as *unpublished*, its author can no longer access it, only being able to access content marked *published*. With this permission, the user can also access his unpublished content, which is necessary for working with drafts.

You might also notice that permissions for reading/viewing specific content types were not present. That is because, while there is a permission for viewing published content, that is as granular as the permissions get for viewing content; there are no permissions regarding viewing a particular content type. There is, however a module that provides those permissions, which we will add in `Chapter 5`, *Making Drupal Even More Useful*. Once we have those permissions available to grant, we can ensure that only the roles we select can comment on a specific content type, because if you can't view the content, you can't comment on it!

Users

We've created the roles specific to our site and assigned to them the permissions that grant them the access that they need. The only thing we're missing now...are users. Each user needs an account. Where do they come from?

There are three ways that most users obtain a Drupal account:

- A user with permissions to create a user account does so on the user's behalf
- The user registers for an account
- The user obtains an account via **single sign-on** (**SSO**), such as through a Facebook account

Of these, the latter method is out of scope for this book, as it is a more in-depth administrative topic. Let's take a look at the other two.

Creating a user account

We're going to learn how to create a user account. Some sites choose to allow users to create an account that immediately becomes active with no review, some choose to require the account to stay inactive until an administrative user approves it, which is what we will emulate here, and some create all user accounts administratively and do not allow users to register.

Let's create an account for an editor, one of the roles we created. If you still have a page up with the tabs for **List**, **Permissions**, and **Roles** at the top, click **List**. Otherwise, you can either click **People** in the **Admin** menu, or navigate to `admin/people`. Here is how we create an account:

1. Click the **+ Add user** button, which will bring you to the **Add user** page, `admin/people/create`.
2. For **Email address**, you can enter a real one if you have it, or a fake one (`@example.com` is a good domain to use for fake email addresses and URLs).
3. The **Username** can be anything. Our editor will be *Edie Editor*, so I'll make her username `Edie`.
4. Choose something you'll remember for a password. The user can change the password once logged in. To get a green bar (strong password) try `Password123`. Enter your choice again in the **Confirm password** field.
5. For **Status**, leave the setting at **Active**. If you ever want to create a user account in advance but not make it immediately active, you would select **Blocked**.
6. Under **Roles**, check the box for **Editor** to give this user that role.

> You'll notice that **Roles** has **Authenticated** selected and that it cannot be unselected. That is because all users with accounts are authenticated, by definition.

7. We're going to leave **Notify users of new account** unchecked. Normally, you would check this so that an email would be sent to the new user, but we do not want an email sent in this case.
8. The **Picture** is nice when there will be something akin to blog articles, where the author has a photo, but we won't use one.

9. Will your content editors want to be contacted via the website? If so, leave the next check box for **Personal contact form** selected.

10. The **Time zone** selection assures that the user sees times displayed based on their time zone, rather than the time zone in which the web server is located.

Having addressed all the fields, click **Create new account**. You will stay on the **Add user** page, with a message similar to the following screenshot at the top:

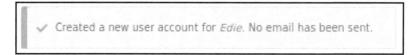

When users are allowed to request an account by registering, there are typically two ways it can be handled, depending on your site configuration: the registration can result in an immediately active account, or the user account will be created as **Blocked** to **Inactive**, until it is approved.

 User registration is configured at **Configuration** | **People** | **Account settings** (`/admin/config/people/accounts`). Learn more at: `https://www.drupal.org/docs/user_guide/en/config-user.html`.

To approve it, you would edit the account from the user list, change the status from **Blocked** to **Active**, and assign the user whichever roles are needed. The only role that will be preselected is **Authenticated**, just as when we created a user.

Summary

We've looked at the major facets of managing users, including roles and permissions. Ensuring that users have the proper roles and that those roles give them access to only the functionality they should have is essential for the security of your content and the site.

Now that we have a site, some content types, and an editor with the proper permissions for working with content, it's time to spend some time on the topic most central to a Content Management System: the content, and that's just what we'll do in `Chapter 4`, *Creating and Editing Content*.

Creating and Editing Content 4

In the preceding chapter we learned about content types. We also learned about designing new content types for specific needs, how to create them, and adding fields to them for storing data and making it available as selection criteria. Now that we've discussed the classification and storage of content, let's switch to the content, itself.

Drupal sites are all about content. In order for the site to present content to the visitor it needs to contain content. How does content get into the Drupal site? In this chapter, you will learn how to work with content, create it and edit it. Throughout this chapter you will create content (for use later in this book), and will learn to do the following:

- Use the WYSIWYG editor
- Configure the editor for other roles
- Navigate the various fields on the content creation form
- Preview content
- Publish content
- Define a custom URL for content
- Add attachments and multiple instances of fields
- Make content stick to the homepage

Using the WYSIWYG editor

When you send a text message from your phone, you type the text, and that's pretty much all there is to it in terms of the content's appearance. You're limited to choosing whether you want to use capital letters. If you want more control over your message, you can switch to sending an email message, which might enable you to select bold, italic, or underlined text.

If you want to send highly formatted content, text with headings, font changes, text color, bulleted lists, and so forth, you might use word processing software, such as Word, Pages, or LibreOffice.

This class of software creates what is called *rich text*, that is, text rich in styling, and the generic term for software capable of creating a document containing rich text is *rich text editor*.

Drupal 8 includes a rich text editor called CKEditor. It is a highly configurable editor with a composition area, as shown in the following screenshot, that resembles standalone word processors with formatting buttons. This type of editor is referred to as **WYSIWYG**, which is pronounced as wizzy-wig, which stands for **What You See Is What You Get**, meaning that the text it displays shows the selected formatting:

Let's create a piece of content and reproduce what is in the image. Click **Content** in the admin menu, then click the **+Add content** button. When you are presented with the list of content types, click **Article**.

Next to the page title, **Create Article**, is a star ☆. If you click it, its outline will become colored, which indicates that the current page has been saved as one of your favorites. You can then navigate to the same page in the future simply by clicking **Shortcuts** in the admin menu and selecting the page title.

The page contains all the fields and settings necessary for creating Article content. Those fields that require an entry have an asterisk following their name, and I will also include an asterisk as we address each of the fields, in turn.

Title*

The *Title* is a required field for all content because it is used to identify one piece of content as distinct from another, though it does not have to be unique, and so more than one piece of content can have the same title, which quickly becomes confusing. The entry in this field will appear in the summary admin list of content. It is also used as the page title when the content is read on its own page. Therefore, it is best to enter a title that is both meaningful to you and informative to the site visitor. Enter one now. Mine will be **A Moment in the Life of My Dog**.

Body

You might be wondering why the *Body* field is not required, since the article would be somewhat useless without body text. It is because you might want to create the article as a draft and return later to actually create the body text. This is not possible with the title, because without one, it would be difficult to find the article.

Summary Field

Next to the field name is a link that reads **Edit Summary**. When creating a content type, the creator decides whether the body text field should accommodate having a separate summary, and if so, that link is shown. The summary is used, for example, when providing a list of content for the site visitor, where a short description of the content—a *teaser*—is provided.

There are two ways to provide the teaser text: via a separate summary or by trimming, that is, excerpting text from the start of the content. I prefer to use the summary because trimmings are based on a set number of characters that is the same for all of the same type of content, such as the first 40 characters, so I have no control over where the excerpt will end... maybe it will end in the middle of a word. With a summary, I can precisely control what will be shown. Even if it is identical to the start of my body text, I am able to ensure that it ends in an appropriate place.

Click the **Edit Summary** link. A Summary text box will appear above that for the body. It contains a link to hide the field again. This toggle of Edit summary/Hide summary allows you to remove its distraction until you need to use it. You will notice that the bottom right corner of the text box has a widget that's meant to resemble page corners that can be grabbed with the mouse and dragged to enlarge or reduce the size of the text box. It also has a note below it letting you know that if you do not enter summary text into the field, Drupal will use a trimmed version of the body text as a summary. Enter some summary text into the field. Mine will read: **Sasha makes an exciting discovery**.

You will notice that below the field is a select box that is set to **Basic HTML**. There are two other settings available by default: **Restricted** and **Full**. Not all user roles will necessarily have all settings available. Each setting allows certain HTML tags, which translates to certain formatting of the text. For more information, click the *About text formats* link.

Body text

In the **Body** field goes the full text of the article. Depending on the text format selected, various buttons are available from the editor for formatting the text. My text looks as follows:

> *Today Sasha Gabor discovered donuts! They're not exactly healthy diet fare for a dog, but she didn't seem to mind.*

Enter some text for your article, and format some of it using the **B** (bold) or *I* (italic) buttons. When you have entered it, click the **Source** button to see what the actual HTML markup looks like. Mine shall look like this:

```
<p>Today Sasha Gabor discovered <strong>donuts</strong>! They're not
<em>exactly</em> healthy diet fare for a dog, but she didn't seem to
mind.</p>
```

If you ever need to customize the underlying HTML of the body text, this is where you can do it. Click the **Source** button again to return to WYSIWYG mode.

Text format

The **Text format** dropdown is used for selecting the filter that will be used when entering text. Security is a constant concern on websites that accept entry from users, as some bad actors will attempt to enter markup that can cause havoc. Filtering which type of markup is allowed helps to mitigate the potential for trouble. These filters can be defined and configured, and the configuration will, for example, identify which HTML tags will be allowed and which processes will be run (such as HTML correction) and in which order. Filters are assigned to user roles, and a user role can have access to more than one filter. The filters that are included with Drupal and their default configurations are as follows:

- **Plain text**: No HTML tags will be accepted
- **Restricted HTML**: A minimal set of HTML such as italics, bold, and headings are typically used for anonymous users (users who are not logged in)
- **Basic HTML**: Similar to Restricted HTML, but usually inclusive of a configuration for WYSISYG toolbar buttons, since the filter is normally used for authenticated (logged in) users who will have access to the editor
- **Full HTML**: Allows any valid HTML tag, and should be assigned with care

This filter will not be included in the dropdown as it is used when no other filters are available.

Tags

The **Tags** field is used to include terms related to the content. These terms can be used by users to search for content. Multiple terms should be separated by commas. The field is an auto-complete field, meaning that any existing terms matching the characters typed will be offered for you to click rather than typing the entire term. My tags will be **Sasha** and **donuts**.

Images

The **Image** field enables choosing a file from the device you are using and uploading it to be stored and associated with the content. The maximum size of the file is given below the field (typically 2 MB) and so are the file types that will be accepted. I'm going to add an image and enter **Sasha and her donut** as alt text. Alt text is used to provide information about the image to those users using a screen reader or some other form of access rather than viewing the image.

INLINE images versus ATTACHMENT images:

Images that are inserted into the text by way of the WYSIWYG editor are treated as part of the text, while images attached to the content by way of the image upload dialog are considered an independent part of the content, like the title, and their visibility can be configured for various contexts, such as teasers, RSS feeds, and so on.

Publishing the content

The **Published** checkbox sets the content's status to be either draft (unchecked) or published (checked). Typically, only editors, admins, and the content's author will be allowed to view the content when in its draft state. The content will not appear in menus or lists to those roles that don't have permission to view it. Let's check the box to publish our content.

Additional settings

That covers the main fields used to create *Article* content. There are additional configuration options available via the vertical tabs. Let's take a look at those:

These additional settings are referred to as metadata, which is information used to describe the content that is not actually part of the content.

Revision log message

If the content type that you are working with is set for revisions, you can enter a description of the changes you have made to the content in this box, and that description will be saved and listed when reviewing the available revisions for this content.

Menu Settings

Should you want a menu link for this content, checking this box will open a dialog for providing the following settings:

- **Menu link title**: The text that appears as a link
- **Description**: The text shown when the mouse hovers over the link
- **Parent item**: The menu link under which this one will be indented
- **Weight**: A value which determines the position of this menu item in relation to any others (based on their weights) with the same parent

Comment Settings

If your content type is set to allow comments, you can set this particular piece of content to accept comments (open) or not (or no longer) accept comments (closed).

URL Path Settings

When a new piece of content is created, it is assigned a sequential numeric ID known as the node ID, or NID. By default, the URL displayed when the content is presented, similar to `http://mysite.com/node/123`, where 123 is the NID. If you want your content to have a more meaningful URL than node/123, such as sasha-discovers-donuts, that custom URL, known as an alias, can be defined here.

When an alias is defined for content, the original URL will still be available for use. You will be able to reach this content using either form of the URL, e.g. https://mysite.com/node/123 or https://mysite.com/my-friendly-content-name.

Authoring Information

If you are creating content on behalf of another user, you can begin typing their username in the text box in this tab and choose the name from the presented matches, as well as specify the date that should be considered the content creation date.

Promotion Options

Content can be "promoted" to a higher status for the purposes of including it on the home page, or even featuring it there.

- **Promoted to front page**: Some sites determine what content is displayed on the front page by selecting only that content that has been promoted.
- **Sticky at top of lists**: If the content is Sticky, it will stay on the homepage while other content is replaced with newer content. This is a good way to have a welcome message remain while other content is cycled.

Completing the process

At this point, we are ready to save our new content by clicking the **Save** button. After doing so, the content is displayed for you to see. Note the URL that is shown. In my case, it is *node/2*. I would rather have something more meaningful for the user and for good SEO, so I will click the **Edit** tab and navigate to the vertical tab for **URL PATH SETTINGS**. There, I will enter /sasha-discovers-donuts (the initial slash is required) and save the article again. Now, the browser will show my improved URL. I can still use the original URL of node/2. It has not been removed. Create a better URL for your content in the same way.

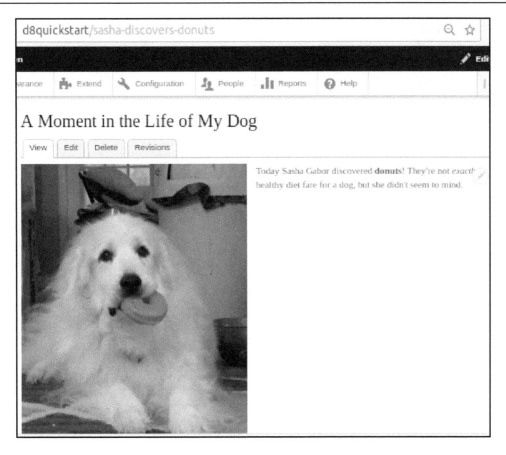

You will notice that one of the tabs above your article reads **Revisions**. Click it. Because the Article content type is configured to create revisions when saved, and we did not override that by unchecking the **Create new revision** checkbox, the change we made and saved in order to improve our URL resulted in the change being saved as a new version rather than simply overwriting the original one. In this manner, we could create a new revision every time we edit the content. From this Revisions page, we can do the following:

- View a list of the previous versions
- View a previous version
- Delete a previous version
- Revert to (restore) an earlier version, foregoing the changes made since

Summary

This brings us to the end of this chapter. Here, we have learned how to create content, use the WYSIWYG editor, configure various options for the content, publish it, make it sticky, save it, edit it, change its URL, and work with revisions.

In the next chapter, we will learn to make Drupal even more useful by extending it with add-on modules.

5
Making Drupal Even More Useful

In the previous chapter we learned how to create content, the mainstay of the Drupal website. Creating content can be accomplished using a simple build-in process. Drupal is fully usable out-of-the-box as a content management without the requirement of any customization. However, your site or business model can call for additional functionality. Perhaps you want to schedule events, or accept payments, or display a product catalog. For this reason, there is a galaxy of add-on features available that can be greatly increase its utility and flexibility.

Perhaps you have added functionality to your browser by way of a browser plugin, or to your smartphone by way of an app. With Drupal, feature expansion is also accomplished by pieces of add-on code, called modules. A module is arranged in a folder that contains program code and other files that, when placed in the correct location within the Drupal folder, provide a feature or service above and beyond those included with Drupal. As is the case with Drupal itself, modules are open source and free of charge, though some serve the purpose of connecting Drupal to a paid, third-party service.

Modules come from one of three sources:

- **Core**: Included with Drupal, sometimes being optional to use
- **Contributed**: Not part of the core Drupal package, but typically made available from Drupal's module library at `https://drupal.org/project/project_module`
- **Custom**: Typically developed specifically for the site on which the module is used

The modules cover a cornucopia of categories, features, and services, from social media integration to image editing and appointment scheduling. This chapter explores a few of the more popular modules that extend Drupal's usefulness for users focused on content. Custom modules are not within the scope of this book. The modules that we will use and look at in this chapter are as follows:

- **Pathauto (contributed, but included with Drupal)**: Automatically generates URI/path aliases for content based on rules created by you
- **Paragraphs (contributed)**: Provides an easy way to add pre-formatted pieces of content to your larger content
- **Content moderation (core)**: Facilitates a process for approving content before it can be published

Pathauto

There are many ways to install modules, and all require some administrative capability. The installation of the contributed module is outside the scope of this book. We'll start from the point of the module files being in the correct place.

Because the **pathauto** module is included with Drupal, the files certainly will be present. We can verify this by navigating to **Extend** on the admin menu, or `/admin/modules`. Once there, enter **pathauto** in the filter text box at the top of the page. You should see the following entry listed:

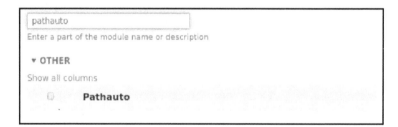

Let's check the box beside it and click the **Install** button. Depending on what other modules have been enabled on your site, you might receive the following message:

If you do receive this message, or a similar one when you are installing a module, it is because the module is dependent on other modules, and one or more of them isn't enabled. If the necessary modules are present, Drupal will offer to enable them as well. Simply click **Continue**. In this case, if all goes well, you will receive a status message at the top of the reloaded page stating that three modules have been enabled: **pathauto**, **Chaos tools**, and **Token**.

At this point, we can configure Pathauto. Most modules have a configuration page, but not all. Scroll down to the Pathauto entry, or use the filter text box to find it, and click the arrow just to the left of the module description. An accordion control will open and reveal a configuration link, among other things. Click it, and you will be redirected to Pathauto's configuration page at `/admin/config/search/path/patterns`. The page will be sparse, because no pattern exists yet. Let's create one.

Click the **+Add Pathauto pattern** button. The resulting page, with the same title as the button that you just clicked, contains a dropdown selection that offers various entity types that are suitable for path patterns. Initially, the option are Content, Taxonomy, Term, and User. For any of those, a path pattern can be specified for creating meaningful URLs. We are going to create a pattern for Content, and select the same.

Our selection causes the page to change a bit, as each content type is now listed. You can check the box for Article, as we are creating a pattern for it.

We need to define the pattern that we want to use. There are many possibilities. We will choose a simple pattern. We'll have article URLs containing the word "content" and the article title in the form `content/my-article-title`. How will we get the article title to be used too? Click the link to **Browse available tokens**.

Tokens are placeholders that will make a specific type of value available at the proper time. A pop-up will appear that contains a number of token categories. We are interested in *Nodes*, so click the arrow beside it. An expanded list will appear, and in it you will find *Title*, referring to the title of the node, or in this case, the article title. To the right of that is a link containing the token for the node title, [node:title]. Click inside the pattern text box, and then click the link for the token. It will appear in the text box. Now, place your cursor to the left of the token and type `content/`.

Lastly, type *articles* in the **Label** text box to identify this pattern. The form should look similar to the following screenshot, though your content type list might vary:

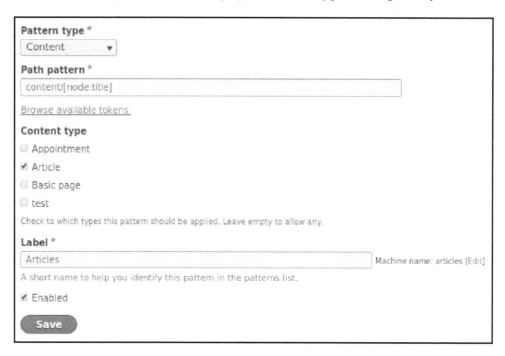

Click **Save** to save your pattern, and you will be returned to the pattern list, which will now have one entry. Let's test it by creating an article. Navigate to `/node/add/article`.

Add whatever title and body text you'd like. I'm naming my article *My New Article*. The magic comes when you save it. When I do, instead of having a URL like `http://d8quickstart/node/5`, I have `http://d8quickstart/content/my-new-article`. Note that the original URL will still exist and can still be used. The Pathauto list at /admin/config/search/path lists both the alias based on the pattern and the original URL for each node. In my case, the node I created has a node ID of 2, and so I could still enter `http://d8quickstart/node/2` as the URL if I so desired.

Notice that Pathauto automatically converted the article title to a URL-friendly string by replacing spaces with hyphens and making the title lower case. The settings for this can be controlled under the **Settings** tab on the Pathauto config page. There is an addition tab there that is very important: **Bulk generate**. Let's say that you create a pattern *after* a number of nodes have already been created. Rather than editing each and changing the URL to match your pattern, you can instruct Drupal to generate a patterned URL for every existing article.

Paragraphs

Paragraphs is a contributed module, which means that it was developed by someone in the Drupal community and was contributed back to Drupal.org. It provides a way to create pre-formatted content that can be easily reused.

Once the files have been deposited in the correct folder, which is typically in `/modules/contrib`, we will enable it as we did Pathauto, via the **Extend** page at `/admin/modules`. You may receive a message indicating that the *Entry Reference Revisions* module must be enabled as well. Simply click **Continue**.

Navigate to **Structure** (`/admin/structure`) and you will see a new entry at the bottom of the list: **Paragraph types**. Click on it, which will bring you to the **Paragraph types** page at `/admin/structure/paragraphs_type`. You will see a message where a list would normally be indicating that there isn't a Paragraph type yet. So, let's create one.

Click on the **+Add paragraph type** button. We're going to create a paragraph type for an image and text, so in the **Label** text box let's enter `Image and text`, and then click **Save and manage fields**. We will need to create two fields for our Paragraph type: one to contain the image, and another for the text.

Click the **+Add field** button. From the select list, choose **Image**. You can enter `Image` as the label, or any value you would prefer. Click **Save and continue**. Leave the settings on the page that follows as is, and click **Save field settings**. On the next settings page, leave those as is too, and click the **Save settings** button.

Click the **+Add field** button once more. Choose **Text** (**formatted, long**) from the select list, and enter **body text** for the label. Click the **Save and continue** button, and the on the following page, click the **Save field settings** button. Finally, click the **Save settings** button. We now have our paragraph type defined.

The list page will look something like it does in the following screenshot:

At this point, we have defined a paragraph type. Now, we need to add it to a content type so that users creating that type of content can use the paragraph type. Let's navigate to **Structure** | **Content types** (/admin/structure/types) and click **Manage fields** beside the **Article** content type.

Click **+Add field** and from the **Add a new field** select list, choose **Paragraph**. For the label, let's enter Paragraph type, and click **Save and continue**. Leave the settings on the following page as is, though make certain that the **Type of item to reference** field has **Paragraph** selected. Click **Save field settings**.

On the next page, **Paragraph type settings**, in the **REFERENCE TYPE** section, we identify which paragraph type(s) should be offered as choices to the content creator. By default, checking a box in the **TYPE** subsection will indicate the inclusion of that type. We also have the option of indicating that any checked box be a type that we want *excluded* from the choices provided to the user. We will use the default method of inclusion, and check the one box available to us, given that we created only a single paragraph type, that is, **Image and text**, as shown in the following screenshot:

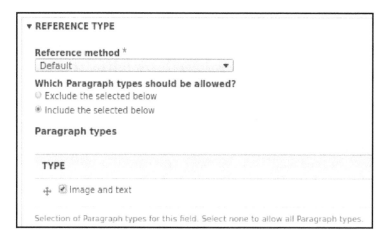

Click **Save Settings**. Now, let's create an article at **Content | Create content | Article** (/node/add/article). Give the article a title. Scroll down and you will see that a **PARAGRAPH TYPE** section has been added, containing the **Image and text** Paragraph type that we created. If we had created additional paragraph types, and marked them to be included as options, they would also be present. In that case, had we decided in creating this article that we wanted to use more than one of the paragraph types, the handle to the left of the type name could be used to drag the types into the order in which they should appear within the content.

Click the **Choose file** button for **Image** and browse to an image to include. Remember to provide alternative text for the image. Then, enter the text that will go with this image into the **body text** box. Note that this field has a WYSIWYG editor available for formatting.

Below the image and text that we've entered is a button that we can use to add another paragraph. If we only wanted the user to be able to add one instance of a paragraph type within a piece of content, we could have changed **Unlimited** to 1 instance in the field settings when creating the field.

Click the **Save** button. When we look at the rendered article, it doesn't look quite like what we had in mind when creating the paragraph type. My image is massive, and both fields have their titles showing. Let's do something about this.

Navigate to **Structure | Paragraphs types** (/admin/structure/paragraphs_type) and select **Manage display** from the select field. Click the settings gear on the right-hand side of the **Image** row. In the select field for **Label**, select **Hidden**, and select **Medium (220x220)** from the one for **Image style**.

You can create additional image styles at admin/config/media/image-styles.

Click the **Update** button to save your changes. Then, in the row for **body text**, select **Hidden** from the **Label** select field. Click the **Save** button.

That takes care of the display settings for the fields *in* the paragraph, but we also want to change a setting for the **Paragraph** field, itself. It, too, displayed its field name, which isn't the behavior we want. So, navigate to **Structure | Content types** (/admin/structure/types) and select **Manage display** from the select field beside **Article**. For the **Paragraph type** field, change the **Label** setting to **Hidden**, and then click **Save**.

Now, when we look at the preview, it is what we had expected: an image on the left with text on the right:

Happy even **without** a donut!

Had we wanted it the other way around, we could edit the **Paragraph type** and swap the order of the image and text fields within it. There is virtually no limit to the number of fields that can be contained with a Paragraph type, nor the number of Paragraph types that can be created.

When you enabled the Paragraphs module, another module listed just below it was Paragraphs library. Enabling that module will enable you to store your created paragraph types in a library of types so that it can be easily selected and reused for other content types.

Having successfully created, edited, and used our Paragraph type, let's move on to the final example in this chapter.

Content moderation

Often, an organization requires the path to published content to be indirect. Rather than the author being able to publish the piece, it must first be moderated, whether by a supervisor, peer, or editor. The *Content Moderation* module introduces the ability to inject moderation into the process of publishing content.

Content Moderation is a module *in core*, meaning that it is included in the main programming code that defines Drupal. Navigate back to the **Extend** page (`/admin/modules`) and enable **Content moderation**. You will receive a message that states in order to do so, *Workflows* must also be enabled.

Let's configure the module. Having enabled it, there is now a new section on the **Configuration** page (/admin/config): **Workflows**. Click that, or navigate directly to /admin/config/workflow/workflows. Here, you will see a content moderation workflow that was created when you enabled the module:

Click **Edit**; here, we will take a detailed look at the sections of a workflow.

States

The term *state* is lacking in context here and therefore can be somewhat ambiguous. For example, if I decide to walk to the store from my home, there are three states:

- Being at home
- Walking to the store
- Arriving at the store

However, state, in the context of workflows, isn't necessarily the same. The default context is that state is synonymous with *static* state. Let's take another look at my example, this time with the states described with further precision:

- Being at home - static
- Walking to the store - transitional
- Arriving at the store - static

States 1 and 3 represent static states – milestones and plateaus – that have been achieved and can remain as such. State 2 is transitional, in that it describes an activity that is occurring to lead from one static state to the next.

In looking at the states, as shown in the following screenshot, all three are static states:

- **Draft**: The content has been, or is in the process of being, created
- **Published**: The content is marked as published and is available to those user roles with permission to view published content of this type
- **Archived**: The content has been published but is now removed from what is considered current material and may or may not be still available for viewing:

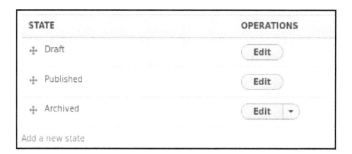

Notice that the Archived state has a select dropdown, while Draft and Published do not. That is because the former is an optional state, which can be deleted using the dropdown, but Draft and Published are not optional.

As you can see, the three states are static. That said, were a transitional state to be needed, it could be created by using the **Add a new state** link.

Let's take a closer look at what constitutes a state. Click on the **Edit** link for **Published**. The name, Published, can be changed if there is a more fitting term for your implementation. The two checkboxes that follow are important:

- **Published**: Whether this term is used for the state, or another if you were to change the State label, checking this box means that when this state is reached, the content is considered published, and the permissions given to each user role with regards to published content apply, typically and particularly in that the content will be available for viewing.

- **Default revision**: In Drupal, if the content type being used has been configured to allow revisions, each time the content is (re)saved, a new revision is created, and anyone with the proper permission can revert the content to an earlier version. If this box is checked, the current version when the state of the content reaches published will be considered the active version.

Next come the transitions. Let's look at **Create new draft**, as its inclusion ~~hear~~ *here* is probably not intuitive. Click on the **Edit** link for it. Again, the label is editable should you have one more suited for your process.

Below the label, you see choices for the *From*, source, state and the *To*, target, state. The target state for this transition is Draft and is not changeable, though were you to create your own transition, it would be. In either case, only one target state can be defined, since *the content can only be in one state at any time.*

More than source state can be selected. The two source states selected might not seem to make sense, given that the target is Draft. However, what events these choices account for are as follows:

- Changing a draft and saving, with it remaining a draft, so **Draft ⇒ Draft**
- Changing published content and saving it, but now as unpublished content needing moderation again, so **Published ⇒ Draft**

A similar peculiarity is true for the transitions of the Publish transition, because you might be (re)publishing already published content, or publishing draft content.

A benefit to this architecture is that while an article is published, a new version of it can be created as a draft and passed through the moderation states until it gets published, becoming the new default—and viewable—version.

Transitions

We have already seen the **Edit** page for a transition, but this section is still worth looking at. You will note that there are multiple transitions defined with the source state being Published, as well as for the source state being Archived. Were you to add a few states, and if each of them could interact with multiple other states, this list of permutations could become lengthy. Not that this is a reason to not define additional states, but simply a mention that more planning might be in order than you might have otherwise thought.

Workflow application

A workflow such as this one needs to have something to act upon. At the moment, this does not apply to any of the content structures available for moderation:

For our purposes, this workflow should apply to all articles, so let's click the **Select** button for Content types. In the resulting pop-up, check the box beside **Articles** and click **Save**. Then, click **Save** for this workflow.

If you create an article now, you might have the option to save it as Draft or Published, as select options at the bottom of the page. If so, this is because you are an administrator or have been given this permission. Otherwise, you will only be able to save the content as draft. Those given the permission to moderate this content or to view it, unpublished, will see the following screenshot when viewing it:

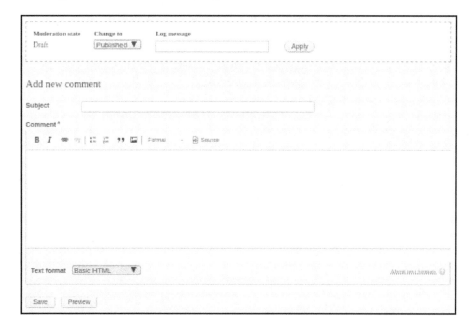

This form allows the moderator to change the state of the content and add a log comment about the transition.

Summary

In this chapter, we have learned what modules are and their utility, their sources, and how to enable them. We have looked at an example of using each of three popular modules to provide capabilities that are not present otherwise.

In the next chapter, we will look at expanding the audience for our content by making it and our site's UI available in more languages via some of the internationalization features of Drupal.

¡Hasta la vista!

Grabbing Global Readership 6

In the previous chapter we learned about expanding the capabilities and features of Drupal. In this chapter we will look at expanding our readership.

The internet makes the world a smaller place. You might create a blog or online store, assuming that your users will be domestic, and be surprised to find that some of them are half a world away. Then, after consideration, you might realize that with most of the world living somewhere outside your own country, global readership can expose your content to many more people.

There is a complicating factor, though. Many of these users—perhaps most—do not speak the same language. You could leave it up to the reader's browser to translate the content, but let's be honest, instantaneous translation such as that provided by Google is problematic at the least with regard to straightforward, unambiguous, dictionary-approved source text, but even more so with colloquial and idiomatic usage.

I often tell the story of a former client who wanted the UI of his English site to be available in Japanese as well. The site sold car parts. The site owner opted for low-budget translation, and that likely resulted in the use of online AI translation. The result was much lower than expected sales. Why? While the translation was fine for menu items such as carburetors and seats, the term used for *Bodies* turned out to mean *Corpses*. Oops!

If a global market is important for the increased usage and success of your site, it is worth having the translation done by those knowledgeable in the two languages and in similar style for both. In other words, using the Queen's English for content and Spanish street slang is probably not your intention. Nor is, again, using Spanish as an example, having the translation be proper Madrid Spanish while your readers are predominantly Latin American.

So you decide to have your content and UI professionally translated. Then what? Do you have to have the equivalent of two sites in order to support two languages?

That is, create separate menus and pieces of content for each? Nope. Drupal has you covered, and just how it does this is what we will be covering in this chapter:

- How to declare additional languages
- How to execute a UI translation
- Entering content translations
- Enabling the user to select a preferred language

When Drupal is installed, the installer selects a default language for the site. In most cases, that language is English. What if there are other languages spoken within our target market? What if our country has more than one official language, or unofficial languages, or English isn't either? The site can be configured to support additional languages, and that is what we must do in order to be able to take advantage of internationalization. To get started, navigate to the **Extend** page (`/admin/modules`).

Scrolling down, you will find the **Multilingual** section:

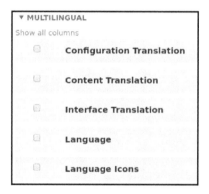

Each of these modules are part of Drupal's core, in core, and has a different purpose related to internationalization:

- **Configuration Translation**: For translating configuration settings, such as views, site name, menus, and blocks
- **Content Translation**: For translating content, such as nodes, taxonomy terms, and custom blocks
- **Interface Translation**: For translating registration forms, content submission forms, and administration interfaces
- **Language**: For declaring additional languages that are usable for translation
- **Language Icons**: For providing flags to represent languages when switching between them

Declaring additional languages

To start, we need to enable the Language module. Check its box and click the **Install** button at the bottom of the page.

In order to declare additional languages, we need to do the following:

1. Enable the language module by checking its box and clicking on the **Install** button at the bottom of the page.
2. Now, when you go to **Configuration** page (`/admin/config`), you will find a section for **Regional and Language**. To start configuring, click **Content language**.
3. Check Content and you will notice that a configuration form will appear, listing each content type. As we are only interested in articles, having a default language as the same would be fine.
4. Check the box to mark the content type as translatable.
5. A list of fields will appear that will belong to Article. Select all of the available fields.
6. After that, check the box that will allow the language to be selected when creating and clicking **Save** configuration.

> In the current version of Drupal (at the time of writing this book), the meta fields should also be selected as translatable. The reason is that if they are not selected, an error will likely be given when trying to save, stating that *Non-translatable fields can only be changed when updating the original language*. This seems to be a bug, because fields that change, such as the creation or update timestamp, are not translatable. This means that they should not have new values, as far as the translation system is concerned.

7. Returning to the **Configuration** page, we will choose **Languages** this time. Note that English is already configured as the default site language.
8. Click **+Add language**. A select box will appear containing a long list of languages. For my site, one of the languages will be **Spanish**, so I'll select that and click to add it. Spanish has now been added, though English remains the default language.
9. Click the **Edit** link for Spanish and change the language name to Español. To me, it makes more sense to display the language name in its own language for those who will be using it. They might not even know what we call their language in English.

Let's add another. This time, I will select **Hebrew**. Once it has been added, click the **Edit** link. You will see in the language definition that **Right to left** is selected, as this is the direction in which Hebrew is written. I'll edit it and translate its name, entering עברית.

That's all there is to declaring languages for use. Now, let's use them and create some multilingual content.

Translating content

In this section, we'll create a short new article to use for our example. Navigate to /node/create/article. For my title, I'll enter **My Favorite Time**. For the body, I've put **Dawn is my favorite time of the day.** Note that below the **Body text** field there is a language selector. Since it is defaulting to **English**, I'll leave it unchanged and save my article. If you still have Content moderation active, don't forget to save your article as **Published** rather than **Draft**.

In order to provide content translations, we need to enable **Content translation**. Let's navigate to **Extend** (/admin/modules) and do that.

With content translation enabled, we have two ways in which to begin a translation: the **Translate** tab, that will now be present beside the **View**, **Edit**, and **Delete** tabs when viewing the content, or, as a **Translate** option via the admin content page, /admin/content, on each Operations selection. Use either to proceed to the translations list for your article.

My translations list looks like this:

LANGUAGE	TRANSLATION	STATUS	OPERATIONS
English (Original language)	My Favorite Time	Published	Edit
Español	n/a	Not translated	Add
עברית	n/a	Not translated	Add

Each piece of content will have rows corresponding to each configured language. The status column identifies whether the content has been translated to that language. If it has, there will be an **Edit** button. If not, there will be an **Add** button. I'll click **Add** in the row for the Spanish translation.

When clicked, the familiar form for editing a node appears. In fact, it appears with the content already filled in for each field. You might think that something is amiss, because there was not supposed to be a translation yet for this language, but there is content instead of empty fields, and it's not the correct language. Don't panic! The content is supposed to be present for you to see what actually needs to be translated, rather than trying to remember. It will appear in the default language. I'm going to translate the title and body text. My form will now look as it does in the following screenshot. Once your translated content seems ready, click the **Save (all translations)** button:

Having saved this translation, the translation list for my content now shows Español, with its translated title, as being published. Next, I'll create a Hebrew translation and save it. The content edit form looks different, because with a right-to-left language, the text fields appear on the right and the metadata fields on the left:

And that's it! The content is now available in three languages (in the next section, we will discuss how a user accesses them).

How does this work behind the scenes? When Drupal stores the field information in the database, part of the index used to find that information is code referring to the language. When you create the content, initially, a node ID—an integer value—is assigned to it. Regardless of how many language translations you create, the node ID remains the same. So, the index for the English version might include the code en for English, es for Spanish, and he for Hebrew.

You might be wondering, how does the user select the desired language? That's what we'll be covering next!

User language selection

Being able to offer content in multiple languages is great, but only if the site visitor can take advantage of it. Drupal makes that easy with a language switcher.

We need to enable another module. Navigate to **Extend** (/admin/modules) and enable the *Language Icons* module. Drupal will let you know that this module depends on the *Interface Translation* module and will ask whether you want to proceed with enabling both. Go ahead.

The Language Icons module provides flag icons for each language. It does this by way of a block that needs to be placed somewhere on the page. Let's do that.

1. Navigate to **Structure | Block layout** (*/admin/structure/block*). You'll need to choose a region of the screen in which to have the language switcher block appear, such as *Header* or *Sidebar first*. I chose the latter.
2. Click the **Place block** button beside whichever region you choose. Scroll down to **Language switcher** and click the **Place block** button in its row. A configuration screen will appear.
3. You can leave the **Title** as **Language switcher**.
4. Uncheck the **Display title** box below it; the icons will speak for themselves without displaying a block title.
5. The vertical tabs allow constraints to be put on this block. The **Language** tab can be used to offer only a subset of the configured languages.
6. The **Content types** tab can limit which types of content the translation will choose. We don't need to set any limitations.
7. If we want to limit the appearance of the **Language switcher** to just the homepage, on the **Pages** tab, we can enter `<front>` into the **Pages** text box.
8. Click the **Save block** button and navigate to the homepage.

On my site, I now have a block that looks like what's shown in the following screenshot. Yours will vary based on the language(s) that you chose:

By clicking on one of the links, the site visitor chooses to receive translated content in that language. Content that's not available in the selected language will not be presented.

Translating the user interface

Now, we know how to provide translated content, but what about the rest of the page, like the menus? A link like **Contact** means little to someone who doesn't speak English. Fortunately, Drupal provides us with the means to translate the UI.

We've already enabled the *Interface Translation* module. We just need to configure it. Navigate to **Config** (`/admin/config`) and click the User interface translation link in the **Regional and Language** section.

So far, the actions that were necessary to provide translated content have been fairly simple. So, you're probably expecting a button to click that will translate all of the prompts and menus in the UI. Sorry... not gonna happen.

The configuration interface allows you to enter a translation string for each string that Drupal finds in the core and modules interfaces. You can use this page, and the many, many, many other pages to translate each, or you can export the list of strings and enter translations all into one file and then import it.

This sounds like a lot of work, and that's because it *is* a lot of work. So, let's look at the easy way to do it. What? You thought I said... no, what I said was that there's no button to translate the interface, but there is an existing translation file for many languages that you can download and import.

1. Navigate to `https://localize.drupal.org/download`. Here, you will find a list of the available UI translation files. In my case, I'm going to download the Drupal 8 version of the file for Spanish and the one for Hebrew. Do the same for the language(s) that you chose. The nice thing about these files is that they are editable, so you can alter strings or add your own when you need new ones, like when you create custom menu links.

2. Next, on the **User interface translation** page, click the **Import** tab at the top of the page.

3. Browse to and select the translation file that you downloaded

4. Select the applicable language from the **Language** dropdown

5. Click **Import**.

I've done this for both languages and the result can be seen in the following screenshots, which shows each version of the homepage when using the **Language switcher** block.

The following screenshot is in Spanish:

And the following screenshot version is in Hebrew, an example of a right-to-left (RTL) language:

This is definitely easier than manually translating every string!

Summary

In this chapter, we've learned how to use Drupal's translation features: configuring additional languages, providing content translations, adding icons that are used by site visitors to switch languages, and importing user interface translations.

In the next chapter, you will learn how to use feeds to import content and to provide your content to other sites.

Feeding the Masses – RSS

7

In this chapter, we will look at what a feed is and how to create one. In fact, we will create two! Here are the topics we will cover:

- Why you would want to provide a feed
- Deciding what content to include in a feed
- Modifying content to enable feed selection
- A brief overview of the Views module
- Using the Views module to create feeds
- Creating a block of feed links

Why feeds?

What is a *feed*? **RSS** stands for **Rich Site Summary**. The word "feed" has many meanings. In our context, the meaning to consider is the one that you've probably heard in regards to broadcast television. For example, there could be an event happening outside London that is being covered by a local network. That network then allows other networks and stations to tap into their continuous broadcast, when desired. That continuous broadcast is referred to as a *feed*, in that it is "food" for another to consume. On the internet, a feed is much the same. A site provides its content in a stream that is pulled (requested) by a site that wants to use that content. That stream is a feed.

Some feeds provide news content. Some are e-commerce feeds that provide products that any registered e-commerce site can sell for a commission. Some simply provide articles on topics of interest to the readers of sites that consume the feeds.

So, why would you want to provide a feed for your site?

Exposure. Providing a feed makes it possible for other sites to consume it and expose your site's content to those who might otherwise never see it.

Selecting content for a feed

What if some of your site content is secure, or available only to premium subscribers? No problem! We're going to look at a way to filter the content selected for the feed, or, conversely, filter out content that you do not want selected.

We're going to create three feeds. The first thing we need to decide upon is what content the feed will contain...which means determining the selection criteria.

One of our feeds is destined for the pet-loving community. It will contain any of our articles related to pets.

Our second feed is for travelers. It will contain any of our articles related to travel.

Finally, our third feed will contain any article that not included in the first two feeds.

Modifying content for feed selection

So, we know what criteria we have for our feeds, but how will Drupal know which content meets that criteria? Let's discuss two possible methods.

Pick-me flags

A *pick-me* flag is a content field that's purpose is to highlight the fact that the content applies to something specific, and so is the flag for selecting it. It is represented by a Boolean field, which contains `True` `(-1)` or `False` `(0)`, so that you can think of it as either on or off. It is typically represented by a checkbox.

So, for our use, we could add a field called Pets to our article content type, and check the box when creating an article if the article touches on pets, and the same with a **Travel** checkbox for travel content.

This makes sense, and is an easy way to determine what content to select, but there is one kink in that plan. Every time a new criterion arises, it would mean adding yet another field to the content type. Things could get messy quickly.

A pick-me flag works best for a standalone need, such as when an article is marked as Published. Fortunately, there is another method available to us.

Tags

Just as content is kept in an entity called a *node*, Drupal also has an entity type called *taxonomy*, which is a scientific word for classification. Just as nodes are represented by content, taxonomy is represented by vocabularies containing terms.

Drupal comes with a taxonomy vocabulary, called **Tags**. The intended use of tags is to categorize content. Additional vocabularies can also be created to hold tags for specific use, such as one for travel-related terms, or one for Spanish-language terms, but for the purpose of assigning categories applicable to the content, this is what the Tags vocabulary was designed for, and it will work for us.

I'm going to go back and edit the article *A Moment in the Life of My Dog*, and in the *Tags* field, which currently contains `Sasha` and `donuts`, I'm going to add one more, `pets`, and save it again.

Then, I will add two additional pieces of content, both related to travel, and will tag them with travel, as well as tags specific to the travel type and destination, as shown in the following screenshots. The following screenshot is related to Iceland:

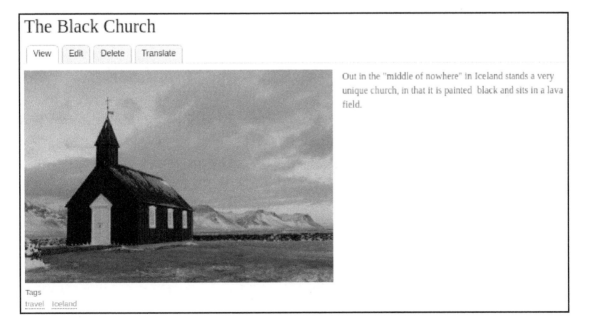

And the other is related to the Caribbean:

Now, we need one final piece of content for the third of our feeds. The tag for this content will be *leftovers*, since the feed is for any content not tagged as **pets** or **travel**.

Having created some content for testing our feed, let's look at how we're going to do that.

Views

Views is a very popular Drupal module. It used to be a contributed module, but is now part of Drupal's core code.

Views provides many features, and so resists a single-sentence description. Rather than trying to describe what it is for, let me give you a simple description of how it works, from which you can infer many of its potential uses.

Views retrieves data from Drupal based on selection criteria and data relationships, arranges it, and outputs it in any number of ways, whether as a component of a Drupal page, as an external file, or as a feed – which is meaningful for our purposes.

To get started, navigate to **Extend** (`/admin/modules`) and enable both **Views** and **Views UI**. The former is the module that provides the services for each view to run, while the latter provides a visual tool for creating views.

Creating the container view

Here, we are going to be creating three feeds. The output choices and displays of the Views module includes both feeds and blocks, and a single view can act as a container for multiple displays. Although we will be creating three view displays, they will all be contained in one view. Let's create it, as follows:

1. Navigate to **Structure | Views** (`/admin/structure/views`) and click the **+Add view** button.
2. In the **View name** text box, we'll enter **Custom RSS Feeds**. I am naming it this way to differentiate it from the predefined RSS view included with the module.
3. Below the name is a checkbox for **Description**. Let's check it, and in the text box that appears, enter `Tutorial examples`. This description will appear in the list of views at */admin/structure/views*.
4. The remainder of the page allows us to provide information in an easy manner that will be carried forward to the **Views UI**, where we can still enter it but with a little more effort. However, we are focusing on creating feeds, and the feed display type is not offered here.
5. Click the **Save and edit** button to save your changes.

Creating the Pets feed

We are now on the Views UI form for our view. The following screen will look slightly different than what you will see, because I have opened the **Advanced** column on the right so that you can see the entire form:

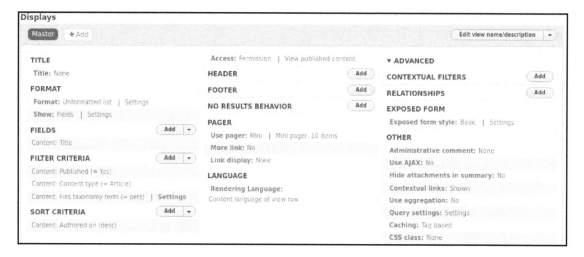

At this point, the only display that exists for our view is the **Master** display, which acts like a template. **Settings** made in it are carried forward to any displays added to the view. Since we will be creating more than one type of display, feeds, and a block, we won't enter the settings on the **Master**.

The first thing we need to do is select the type of display we want. Most often, this will be a page or a block, but we want to create a feed. Click the **+Add** button at the top and select **Feed** from the list. Now that a display has been added, the Master display will be hidden and replaced with Feed. The asterisk is present because the display has been modified but not yet saved.

Let's work our way through the settings, one panel at a time.

Display name

The display name is currently **Feed**, which would be fine if we were to only have one in the view. Since we will be having three, we'll make the name more specific. Click the word **Feed** and enter `Pets Feed` in the popup, and then click **Apply**.

Title

We want to add a title, so click None, and in the popup, enter `D8QuickStart Pets Feed`, and then click **Apply**.

Format

We want the format to be an RSS feed, so that can be left as is. Click the **Settings** link and enter the same string that we used for the feed title, that is, **D8QuickStart Pets Feed**. We don't have to use the same one, but it provides a descriptive title that also works to describe the RSS content. Click the **Apply** button.

Feed settings

I'm going out of order for a moment. The reason for this is that Views provides a live preview area that shows what the view output will be based on what settings have been entered. This preview is at the bottom of the page, but if you scroll down, you will just see an error telling you that the feed should have a path, but none has been supplied. As long as an error is present, no preview will be generated, so let's get rid of the error.

We'll make our path `/pets/feed`. Click **Path** and enter that into the text box in the popup, click **Apply**, and click **Save** at the bottom of the page.

Scrolling down to the Preview area, you will now see a preview of the feed. It might look a bit strange, but an RSS reader will know what to do with it. But all of our content is there...not just articles about pets. Let's address that next.

Filtering the criteria

We're skipping the **Fields** pane because we're not going to be specifying specific fields. We'll let Views parse our article content itself.

Regarding **Content Published**, there may be circumstances where unpublished content should be included in the feed, but this isn't one of those times. Views has set this to **Yes** to show only published content.

The next filter we want to put in place will be to limit the select to Articles. Click the **Add button** and type **Content type** in the **Search** text box. The list of filter criteria will be filtered to just that one, and we'll check the box next to it.

While we're at it, let's also enter the criterion that will allow us to select only articles about pets. Clear the **Search** text box and enter Tax. From the resulting list, check the box for **Has taxonomy term**, and then click the **Add and configure filter criteria** button.

The first popup is for specifying what content types we want included in our feed. Since we only want Articles, we'll check that box, then click **Apply and continue**.

The next popup is used to select the taxonomy vocabulary that will contain the term(s) to which we will limit the content. Since Tags is the only vocabulary we have, it is already selected. Click **Apply and continue**. In the subsequent popup, enter pets into the text box and click **Apply**.

Now, when we scroll down to the Preview area, the only content present is the *A Moment in the Life of My Dog* article.

Sort criteria

There is only one criterion present, but it is the one we want. The content will be ordered based on its creation date, with the most recent coming first.

With that, we've completed our first feed. To test it, you will need to have a RSS feed reader installed in your browser. Given that, and entering /pets/feed, we can see that the feed works as it should:

Feed preview

A Moment in the Life of My Dog
A Moment in the Life of My Dog ayen Wed, 07/18/2018 - 17:14

Let's click **Save** and move on to our next feed.

Creating the Travel feed

Our Travel feed will be much like the Pets feed. One thing we would like to do differently is have the feed include the image that is part of the content, because travel consuming sites are very visually focused.

Since we have already created a feed display, we can clone it and make the changes we need rather than starting from scratch. Find the drop-down that reads **View Pets Feed** and click the arrow, and then click **Duplicate Pets Feed**.

You will note that we now have two **Pets Feed** listings in the **Displays** pane. The highlighted one is the new one. Let's quickly change its name before we get confused by both having the same name. Click the link for **Pets Feed** beside **Display name** and change the name to `Travel Feed` before clicking **Apply**.

Title

We will make the same change to the **Title**, changing **Pets** to `Travel`, but before clicking **Apply**, ensure that you change the drop-down from **All displays** to **This feed (override)**, which will change the text of the **Apply** button to **Apply (this display)**, otherwise you will change both feeds:

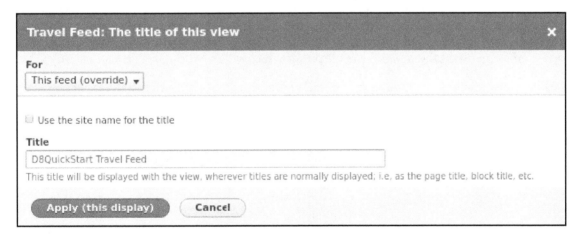

When working with more than one display, be careful when making settings changes to ensure that the change is configured properly, either for only the display you are currently editing, or for all displays, if that is your intention. Accidentally applying a change to all displays (the default) can result in a lot of extra work. The easiest way to remember this is to always note what the **Apply** button says.

Feed settings

I'm going out of order again. This time, we need to change the path, which has been copied from the Pets feed.

We'll make our path /travel/feed. Click **Path** and enter that into the text box in the popup, and click **Apply**.

Format

Make the same change under **Settings** in the **Format** section, by changing **Pets** to **Travel**. You will notice that this setting does not offer the choices that we just discussed. Some settings apply only to a single display.

We're going to change things up somewhat in order to accommodate our need for having the content image included in the feed. Let's tell Drupal that we want the feed to be in a different format than the default, the output of which you saw for the Pets feed.

Beside **Show**, click *Use site default RSS settings* and from the popup select **Teaser**. A content teaser typically contains text and an image—if the content contains one—and that is what we want. Click the **Apply** button.

Filtering criteria

We're skipping the **Fields** pane because we're not going to be specifying specific fields. We'll let Views parse our article content itself.

Only one setting from the Pets feed needs to be changed. Click the **Has taxonomy term (= pets)** link . In the subsequent popup, enter travel into the text box, select **This feed (override)** in the dropdown at the top, and click **Apply (this display)**.

Now, when we scroll down to the Preview area, we will be able to see our feed with teasers of our travel content:

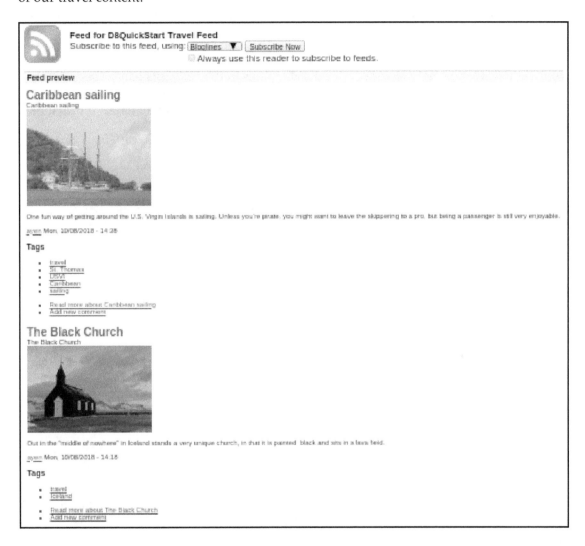

Two down and one to go!

Creating the Leftovers feed

We will clone the Pets feed, since it doesn't include images and neither will this one. Click the **Pets Feed** button in **Displays** to switch to it from the **Travel Feed**. Find the drop-down that reads **View Pets Feed** and click the arrow, and then click **Duplicate Pets Feed**.

You will note that we now have two **Pets Feed** listings in the *Displays* pane. The highlighted one is the new one. Let's quickly change its name before we get confused by both having the same name. Click the link for **Pets Feed** beside **Display name** and change the name to `Leftovers Feed` before clicking **Apply**.

Title

We will make the same change to the **Title**, changing **Pets** to `Leftovers`, but before clicking **Apply**, ensure that you change the drop-down from **All displays** to **This feed (override)**, which will change the text of the **Apply** button to **Apply (this display)**, otherwise you will change all feeds.

Feed settings

We'll make our path `/leftovers/feed`. Click **Path** and enter that into the text box in the popup, and then click **Apply**.

Format

Make the same change under **Settings** in the **Format** section, changing **Pets** to `Travel`.

Filtering criteria

Click the **Has taxonomy term (= pets)** link. In the subsequent popup, change **Is one of** to **Is none of**. Enter **travel** into the text box after **pets**, separating them with a comma, select **This feed (override)** in the drop-down at the top, and click **Apply (this display)**.

Now, when we scroll down to the Preview area, we will see our final feed containing all content other than the content that was used for the first two feeds.

Great! We've finished with our view. Let's create the menu block!

Creating the Feed Links block

Our feeds won't be of much use if site visitors can't find them, so we will create a means for them to do so. We're not going to be using Views for this. You might wonder why, since Views can create a block display. Views is made to select items (rows of data) and create an output for each, whether that be feed items, pages of articles, or a bulleted list. Our links are going to be HTML text unrelated to rows. In other words, this is one block of text without any regard to a selection of article content or any other content. Because of that, the easiest approach is to create a custom block to act as a feed menu on the home page, like so:

1. Navigate to **Structure** | **Block layout** (`/admin/structure/block`) and click the tab for **Custom block library**. Then, click the **+Add custom block** button.
2. For the **Block description**, enter `RSS feeds`.
3. For the **Body**, click **Source** in the toolbar, and then enter the following:

```
<a href="/pets/feed">Pets</a><br />
<a href="/travel/feed">Travel</a><br />
<a href="/leftovers/feed">Other topics</a>
```

4. Click **Source** again, then click **Save**.

Summary

In this chapter, we have learned what RSS feeds are and how they are used, and how to create content meant for a feed. We have learned about the Views module and what views are, how to create a view with multiple feed displays, and how to create a block menu.

In our final chapter, we will put everything together in a home page, including making use of the block we created in this chapter.

8
Welcome Home!

So far in this book, we've learned about many of the things that can be done to quickly get a Drupal site up: creating content types, fields, and content; managing users; adding modules; providing translations; and creating feeds for other sites to consume. With all of these topics, there are still a few left to cover, and that becomes evident when we look at our home page.

BAD home page!

There are many things about our home page that are bad, as shown in the following screenshot:

Some, the design-related ones, are out of the scope of this book, but there are others that we can address. Let's make a list of what's bad about our home page:

- Too much content!
- There is no access to the content that is not on the home page
- Our RSS feeds menu needs to be added
- The footer menu says Legal instead of **Terms and Conditions**
- The Legal link leads back to the home page

Design improvements

Next, let's take our list and consider the deficiencies and what can be done to remedy them.

Too much content!

Drupal is a content management system, of course, but that doesn't mean that all the content should be on the home page. It becomes too long and cluttered. It's better to show only one complete piece or a small number of teasers.

There is a view that provides the selection of content for the home page. Its default behavior is to include all content that has been promoted by checking its **Promote to front page** checkbox. So, we could limit the number of pieces displayed by limiting the number of those promoted. Let's be a little more creative.

We will limit the teaser to the most recent piece of promoted content and create a block that offers the others as a list of links.

No access to content

This is the opposite problem of the first one. If we're going to show the most recent piece of content, and a handful of others in a list, what about the content that is older than that? This is a dilemma suited for the same solution you often see with a blog: an archive. We'll create one to show the older content.

No RSS feeds menu

This is an easy one to resolve. We have already created a custom block that provides a menu for our RSS feeds. All we will need to do is place this block on the home page.

We need a Terms and Conditions page

The footer menu has a **Legal** link, which leads back to the home page. We'll change it to the heading we want, and create a page to link to it.

Making the changes

Now that we have a plan, let's get busy!

Improving the Frontpage view

Navigate to **Structure** | **Views** (`/admin/structure/views`). Scroll down to the **Frontpage** view. This is one of the views that comes with Drupal. We could modify it, but it is a good practice to leave the original unchanged and, instead, make a duplicate to modify, which is what we'll do here:

1. From the drop-down in its row, select **Duplicate**.
2. In the **View name** text box that then appears, change the name to `Frontpage - Custom` and click **Duplicate**.
3. On the **View** configuration page, we will change the number of items that the view displays. It is currently configured to show 10 items and a pager, but we will change it to show only one. Click **Full** and select **This page (override)** from the drop-down. Select the setting for **Display a specified number of items**, and click **Apply (this display)**.
4. In the **Pager options** dialog, change the **Items per page** to `1`, click **Apply**, and then click **Save**.
5. Return to the views list at `/admin/structure/views`. If you look at the list, you will see that the original **Frontpage** and our **Frontpage - Custom** both have the same path.

6. The path needs to be /node for technical reasons, but we cannot have two views responding to the same path. Therefore, in the row for the original Frontpage, select **Disable** from the drop-down.

7. This change will ensure that only the most recent piece of content. Let's edit our new view so that we can add an additional display to it. The current display is for the home page, but we also want a display that provides a block of title links for additional content.

8. On its configuration page, click the **+Add** button in the **Displays** panel, and select **Block**.

Title

Click on the link for **Title**, and select **This block (override)** from the drop-down. Then, in the pop-up, enter Recent articles, and click **Apply (this display)**.

Format

Click the **Content** link and select **This block (override)** from the drop-down. Then, select **Fields** and click **Apply (this display)**. In the subsequent pop-up, click **Apply**.

Fields

At this point, we have told **Views** that we want our output to be a list, and that we want to be able to select the **fields** that will be in that list, but we have no fields selected. Views doesn't like that, and it doesn't help us, giving us an empty output. Let's let Views know that we want a list of titles that link back to the content.

Click the **Add** button. select **This block (override)** from the drop-down, scroll down and check the box for **Title**, and then click **Apply (this display)**. In the subsequent pop-up, click **Apply (this display)**.

Filtering criteria

There are number of filters in effect, but we want to also filter on the content type, limiting it to **Article**.

Click the **Add** button, select **This block (override)** from the drop-down, scroll down and check the box for **Content type**, and then click **Apply (this display)**. In the subsequent pop-up, check the box for **Article**, and click **Apply (this display)**.

Block settings

Click **None** next to **Block name**, enter `Recent articles` in the text box, and click **Apply**.

Pager

Click **10 items**, change `10` to `3`, set the offset to `1`, and click **Apply**. This tells Views that the three most recent articles after the most recent should be used. The reason we ignore the most recent is that it is the one that will appear as a teaser in the main content area, so we don't want to have its title appear in the block as well.

That completes our block. Don't forget to click **Save**.

Navigate to **Structure** | **Block layout** (`/admin/structure/block`). In the **Sidebar first** section, click **Place block**. Then, in the row for **Recent articles**, click **Place block**, and then click **Save block**.

Adding an Archive

Navigate to **Structure** | **Views** (`/admin/structure/views`), scroll down to the **Disabled** section, and enable the **Archive** view.

Navigate to **Structure** | **Block layout** (`/admin/structure/views`), in the **Sidebar first** section. Then, click **Place block**, and scroll down in the row for **Archive**. Here, click **Place block**, and then click the **Save block** button.

Adding the RSS Feeds menu

Earlier, we created a RSS feeds block display in a view. Let's add that block to our home page now.

Navigate to **Structure** | **Block layout** (/admin/structure/views). In the **Sidebar first** section, click **Place block**. Then, scroll down the row for **RSS Feeds**, click **Place block**, and finally click the **Save block** button.

Fixing the Footer menu

We want to fix the Legal link. One of the things we need to fix is that it is currently linking to the home page rather than a Terms and Conditions page. Drupal will not allow a path to be specified for the menu item unless the path already exists. Therefore, we need to create a Terms and Conditions page first.

Navigate to **Content** | **Create content** (/node/add) and select **Basic page** as the content type. In the **Title** text box, enter Terms & Conditions. We're not going to enter the legalese at this point, but let's type Placeholder in the **Body** field for now. Click the vertical tab for **URL Path Settings**, enter /termsandconditions, and click **Save**.

Navigate to **Structure** | **Menus** (/admin/structure/menu) and click the **Edit** menu button for the **Footer** menu.

Click the **Edit** button for the Legal link, and change the title from Legal to **Terms & Conditions**. For the Link, type Terms, and then when the autocomplete field offers the content title, click it. Enter T's & C's in the **Description** text box and click **Save**.

This completes our improvements.

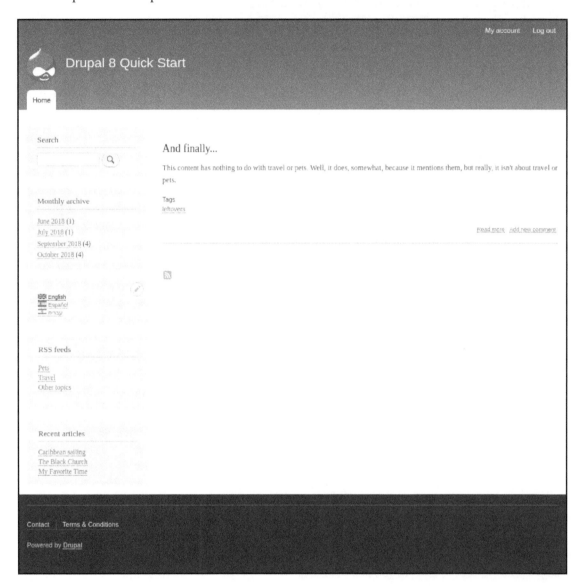

Summary

In this chapter, we learned how to improve a weak home page by editing its view, providing an archive and recent content block, and change the footer menu.

This completes *Drupal 8 Quickstart*. I hope this book has helped you get your site up and running as well as helped your understanding of basic Drupal features. Thanks for reading!

Other Books You May Enjoy

If you enjoyed this book, you may be interested in these other books by Packt:

Drupal 8 Module Development
Daniel Sipos

ISBN: 978-1-78216-877-5

- Write a Drupal 8 module with custom functionality and hook into various extension points
- Master numerous Drupal 8 sub-systems and APIs
- Model, store, and manipulate data in various ways and for various purposes
- Display data and content in a presentable and secure way
- Learn about the theme system and render arrays

Mastering Drupal 8

Chaz Chumley, William Hurley

ISBN: 978-1-78588-597-6

- Write a Drupal 8 module with custom functionality and hook into various extension points
- Master numerous Drupal 8 sub-systems and APIs
- Model, store, and manipulate data in various ways and for various purposes
- Display data and content in a presentable and secure way
- Learn about the theme system and render arrays

Leave a review - let other readers know what you think

Please share your thoughts on this book with others by leaving a review on the site that you bought it from. If you purchased the book from Amazon, please leave us an honest review on this book's Amazon page. This is vital so that other potential readers can see and use your unbiased opinion to make purchasing decisions, we can understand what our customers think about our products, and our authors can see your feedback on the title that they have worked with Packt to create. It will only take a few minutes of your time, but is valuable to other potential customers, our authors, and Packt. Thank you!

Index